Fundamental Method for
MALLETS

MITCHELL PETERS

ABOUT THE AUTHOR

Mitchell Peters joined the Los Angeles Philharmonic in 1969 where he currently serves as principal timpanist and percussionist. Prior to his appointment to the Los Angeles Philharmonic, he was principal percussionist with the Dallas Symphony Orchestra.

Mr. Peters has performed on numerous recordings with both the Los Angeles Philharmonic and the Dallas Symphony, in addition to numerous motion picture and television sound tracks. He is also a member of the Philharmonic New Music Group and has recorded a wide array of contemporary works as a chamber musician.

Mr. Peters holds the Performer's Certificate and bachelor's and master's degrees from the Eastman School of Music, where he studied with William Street. While at Eastman, he was a member of the original "Marimba Masters." Upon graduation, Mr. Peters served as timpanist with the Seventh U.S. Army Symphony Orchestra.

A widely published author and composer, Mr. Peters's compositions and instructional materials are highly regarded throughout the United States and abroad. He currently owns and operates a music publishing company that handles percussion works exclusively.

Mr. Peters is the Percussion Instructor at UCLA where, in addition to teaching privately, he conducts the Percussion Ensemble. He is also on the faculty of the Music Academy of the West in Santa Barbara.

PREFACE

The goal of this book is to provide musical and technical studies which will aid in the development of a solid foundation in the playing of the mallet percussion instruments.

This book has been written with the assumption that the student already has some knowledge of music, possibly through the study of other percussion instruments, or at least has had some type of basic music instruction. The help of a good percussion teacher is highly recommended.

If possible, it is suggested that the beginner start on a marimba. The transfer of technique from the marimba to the other keyboard instruments is easy, and there is an abundance of instructional material and literature available for the marimba. In addition, the larger range of the marimba provides the student with more technical and musical possibilities, particularly when the use of four mallets is employed.

The author has attempted to keep the bulk of the studies and exercises within a limited range, so that any of the keyboard instruments (xylophone, vibraphone or even bells) could be used for practicing, in the event a marimba is not available.

This method is divided into two volumes, both with two distinct parts: Part I, which deals with basic two-mallet technique, and Part II, which deals with four-mallet technique. In Book 1, it is the author's intention that Part II should be started while working on Part I, soon after the student has developed a good control of basic two-mallet playing.

In Book 1, Part I covers major scales through four flats and four sharps, minor scales through two flats and two sharps, chromatic scales, double stops, and other basic two-mallet technique; Part II covers basic four-mallet technique and presents some simple four-mallet studies.

In Book 2, Part III covers the remaining major and minor keys, while Part IV continues to expand four-mallet technique with more advanced technical studies and etudes. Vibraphone technique is also discussed.

The learning of all the major scales and chords as quickly as possible is highly recommended. All the technical studies, no matter which key they are presented in, can be transposed to all other major and minor keys. The fact that a particular exercise is in a particular key is not meant to imply that the exercise is common to that key. The author has attempted to provide a variety of patterns involving numerous keys, rather than presenting the same patterns in every key (except for the Basic Patterns). Additionally, the technical patterns progress in difficulty as the book progresses.

As with most other endeavors in life, becoming a good mallet player will require a commitment of time and energy, as well as consistent practice and patience.

ACKNOWLEDGMENTS

I wish to thank Dave Black (Acquisition/Project Editor), Joel Leach (Percussion Consultant), Jennifer Judkins, Kathy Dayak, Susan Christiansen and J. Jeff Leland (Photographer) for their assistance.

NOTATION

Music for keyboard percussion instruments is usually written in the treble clef. The bass clef is also used frequently for the marimba and occasionally for the chimes. The mallet player must be familiar with both clefs.

Treble Clef

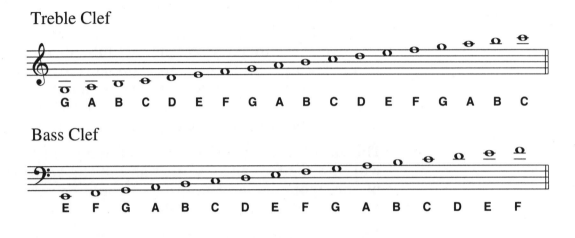

It is not uncommon for a marimba solo work to be written using both clefs simultaneously, as in piano music.

Grand Staff (Combining Treble and Bass Clefs)

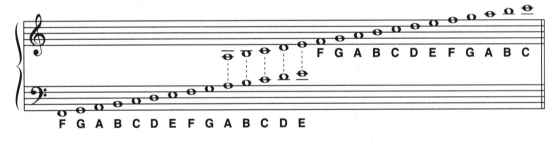

Example of marimba piece using both clefs.

MALLET-PLAYED KEYBOARD PERCUSSION INSTRUMENTS

The pitched percussion instruments whose bars (or tubes, in the case of the chimes) are arranged chromatically, the same as the piano keyboard, have become known as "keyboard percussion instruments" or "mallet instruments."

The most common "mallet instruments" are the xylophone, marimba, orchestra bells, vibraphone and chimes. The xylophone and marimba both have bars made of hard wood, but the tone quality of these two instruments is quite different. The xylophone is brilliant and piercing, while the tone of the marimba is mellow and resonant.

The bells and vibraphone have bars made of metal. The chimes employ metal tubes suspended vertically which are struck with a hammer-shaped mallet.

Unfortunately, few of the mallet instruments have been standardized in range. That means that marimbas can, for instance, be found in sizes ranging from 2 1/2 octaves to 5 octaves. Similarly, the bar sizes (length, width and thickness) also vary depending upon the manufacturer.

There are many technical fundamentals which are applicable to the playing of *all* the keyboard instruments, with the exception of the chimes. There are, however, specific musical and technical practices which are unique to each instrument.

Book I will focus on the basic musical and technical aspects of playing that can be applied to all of the above instruments.

XYLOPHONE

The bars of the xylophone are traditionally made of rosewood, though bars made of synthetic materials have become popular in schools, because of their durability. However, the properly aged wood bars have a far superior tone quality.

The sound of the xylophone is very brilliant and piercing. The xylophone produces sounds of shorter duration than does the marimba because of the xylophone's higher register and thicker bars.

The xylophone is used frequently in orchestral and band repertoire to accentuate rapid passages. It almost always has resonators and is usually played with hard rubber-, wood- or plastic-headed mallets.

Though there has been no standardization of the range of the xylophone, the most common range is 3 1/2 octaves (F4 to C8). It sounds one octave higher than it is written. (This avoids the use of many ledger lines.) There are many different sizes and ranges of xylophones in existence.

Photo courtesy of Yamaha Corporation of America

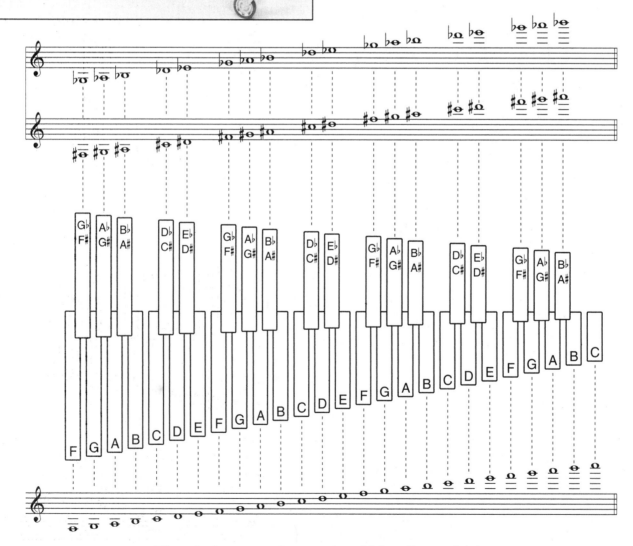

The xylophone sounds one octave higher than written.

MARIMBA

The marimba is the most popular solo instrument of the keyboard percussion instruments, due to its wide range and warm, resonant tone. It is not used as frequently as the xylophone in orchestra and band literature, because it does not project through a large group of instruments as well as the xylophone does.

The bars of the marimba are usually made of rosewood, and are cut wider and thinner than those of the xylophone. The marimba always has resonators. It can be played with a wide array of mallets, usually yarn, cordwound or rubber. Be careful not to play the marimba with mallets that are too hard, because they will not produce the characteristic sound of the marimba and can damage the bars and affect the tuning.

The notes of the marimba sound at written pitch. There is no standard range for the marimba. Through the years, marimbas have been manufactured ranging in size from 2 1/2 to 5 octaves. The most common size today is 4 1/3 octaves (A2 to C7), but many solo performers are using 4 1/2- and 5-octave marimbas.

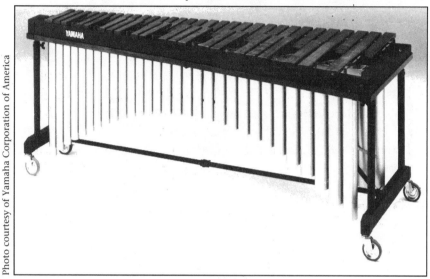

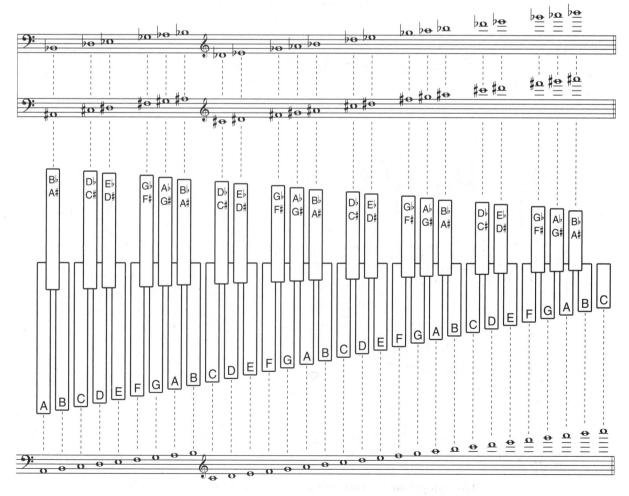

The marimba sounds at written pitch.

ORCHESTRA BELLS (GLOCKENSPIEL)

Orchestra bells are used frequently in orchestra and band literature. The bars of the orchestra bells are made of metal (usually tempered steel) and are normally played with hard rubber, plastic or brass mallets. For softer passages, sometimes a medium-hard rubber mallet can be used. Most models of orchestra bells manufactured today do not have resonators, although deluxe instruments with resonators are available. Orchestra

bells do not articulate well in rapid passages. The tones ring strongly, and if notes are written too rapidly the sound becomes very unclear. The range of orchestra bells varies, but the most common range manufactured today is 2 1/2 octaves (G5 to C8). Orchestra bells sound two octaves higher than written.

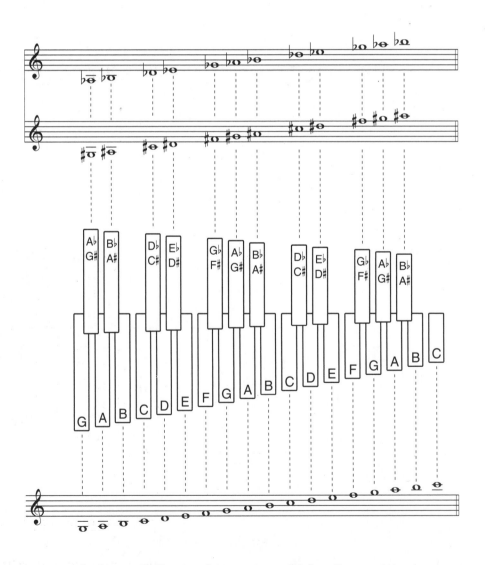

Orchestra bells sound two octaves higher than written.

VIBRAPHONE

The bars of the vibraphone are made of a metal alloy. The standard range of the vibraphone is three octaves (F3 to F6) and it is usually played with yarn or cord-wound mallets. (Hard rubber, plastic, wood and metal mallets will damage the bars.) The vibraphone sounds at written pitch.

The vibraphone has a foot-operated damper pedal, which is used to control the duration of the tone, much like the sustaining pedal on the piano.

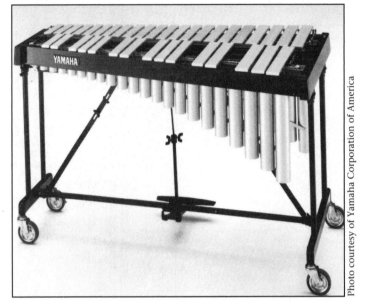

The vibraphone also employs metal discs located inside the resonators. These discs are attached to a rod which turns by means of electric power, causing the discs to open and close the resonating tubes. This action creates a vibrato effect; hence, the name vibraphone. The vibraphone has become very popular in jazz both as a solo and ensemble instrument.

Photo courtesy of Yamaha Corporation of America

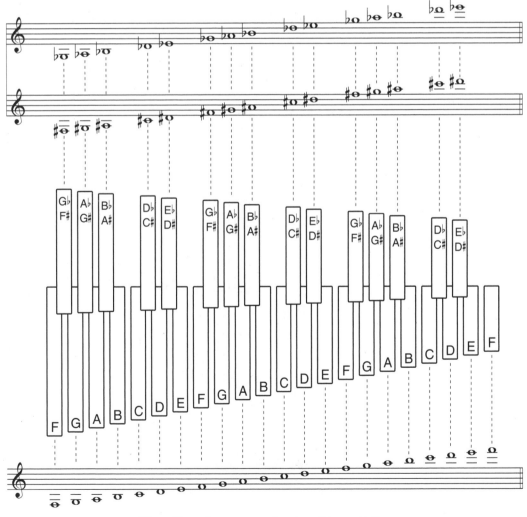

The vibraphone sounds at written pitch.

CHIMES

Instead of horizontally mounted bars, chimes consist of suspended metal tubes which are capped at the top. The chime's tubes are struck at the top on the side of the cap, with the mallet angled slightly, so that it doesn't strike the tube flat. Most passages are playable with one mallet, but some require two.

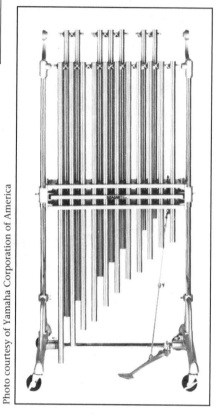

Photo courtesy of Yamaha Corporation of America

The normal range is 1 1/2 octaves (C to F). The chimes sound at written pitch, although their complex harmonic series (consisting not only of overtones, but also a variety of undertones) sometimes makes it difficult to discern the true pitch and register of the note one hears.

Most chimes are equipped with a dampening pedal which controls note duration. (Most muffle when depressed, a few work in the reverse.)

The chimes sound at written pitch.

THE BARS

The bars of mallet percussion instruments are arranged chromatically, the same as the keys of the piano. The lower, or unbroken, row of bars, called *naturals,* are the same as the piano's white keys; while the upper, or broken, row of bars, called *accidentals* (sharps and flats), are the same as the piano's black keys.

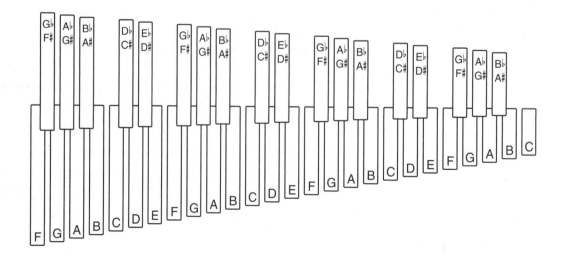

The bar sounds the best when struck in the center, directly above the resonator. However, for fast technical passages it is helpful to strike the sharps and flats on the ends of the bars (the ends nearest the natural notes). This will minimize movement and facilitate technique for fast passages. Be sure to strike the bar on top of the very end of the bar, staying away from the nodal point where the suspension cord passes through the bars. When playing on the ends of the accidental bars it may be necessary to strike the natural bars slightly off center, toward the accidentals, to balance the sound.

When the passage is not rapid, strike the sharps and flats in the middle of the bar over the resonator. Except for a very rare effect, one should never strike the bars over the area where the cord passes through them.

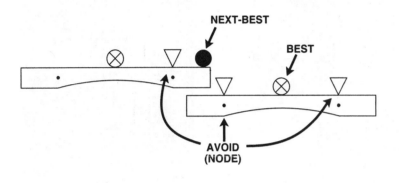

Where to strike the bars.

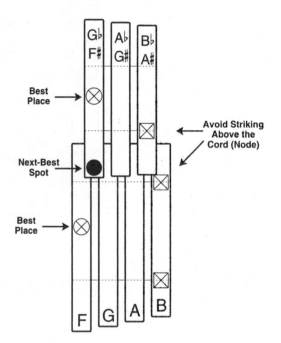

SELECTION OF MALLETS

Each of the mallet percussion instruments can be played with a variety of different mallets, depending on the sound or color desired. The choice of mallet has a substantial effect on the resulting sound.

Ultimately the player will need a variety of mallets, but begin with a pair of medium yarn or rubber mallets. Mallets which are neither extremely soft nor extremely hard will bring out the tone and warmth of the instrument.

THE BASIC TWO-MALLET GRIP

The development of a proper mallet grip is extremely important to the development of good mallet technique. The mallet is held the same way in each hand, in a manner similar to the matched grip used when playing the snare drum. The mallet should be held between the first joint of the index finger and the thumb, with the remaining three fingers curled very lightly around the shaft of the mallet. The thumb should be on the side of the handle, with the palm of the hand facing downward. The mallet should be held approximately two-thirds of the distance from the ball of the mallet. Hold the mallet with a relaxed grip; if it is held too tightly, a resonant tone will not be produced.

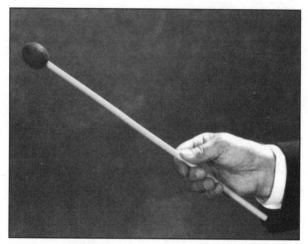

Keyboard mallet grip, palm to the side.

*Keyboard mallet grip,
palm down.*

PLAYING POSITION

Ultimately the position of the body will vary, depending upon what instrument you are playing and the range being covered. A xylophone part played with two mallets and covering a range of two octaves will have to be approached differently than a complex marimba solo covering a 4-octave plus range. Try to be natural and comfortable in your position.

The beginner should start by positioning the body in the middle of the instrument, or more properly, in the middle of the range being played. Body weight should be distributed evenly between the feet, which should be spread apart slightly (about 12"). Don't stand too close to the instrument: position yourself approximately six inches away. The body should lean slightly toward the instrument.

When it is necessary to change position, slide the feet from side to side, rather than by crossing the feet. It is often more helpful to pivot from the waist and lean over the instrument, rather than reposition the body.

The forearms should be approximately parallel to the floor but with a slight downward angle. It may be necessary to adjust the height of the instrument in order to be physically comfortable. On some instruments this can be achieved by means of a height adjustment mechanism. Most instruments, however, lack such a device, so it may be necessary for taller students to place blocks of wood under the wheels in order to raise the instrument to a more comfortable playing height.

Keyboard mallet grip in playing position.

When playing, keep the hands low and close to the keyboard. The hands should be close enough to the keyboard so that by extending the back fingers (the fourth and fifth fingers), you can touch the bars. Place the left mallet slightly in front of the right mallet for most playing. There should be approximately a 90-degree angle between the mallets' handles when in proper playing position. As you move up and down the instrument, the position of the arms will change, but try to maintain a 90-degree angle between the mallets.

Hand distance from bars.

When standing in the center of the instrument while playing at its low end, the player will quite naturally reverse the placement of the mallets; i.e., the right mallet will then be in front of the left—an exception to the basic rule stated above.

Playing position in lower register.

THE STROKE

The basic stroke action is a relaxed up and down motion which should be executed almost entirely from the wrist with the arms and shoulders relaxed. The height of the stroke will vary in relation to its dynamic level, but for the beginning student a stroke of 6" to 8" is recommended as a starting point. As one begins to play faster, the size of the strokes will decrease. Avoid excessive and unnecessary motion.

The actual motion of the stroke is down and up, rather than up and down. (Some refer to this as the "down-up stroke" or "piston stroke.") Place the mallet head on the bar to be struck. The handle of the mallet should now be parallel to the floor. Using the wrist, raise the mallet off the instrument about 6" to 8". This is the actual starting and ending position for the stroke. To execute a stroke, strike the bar and return immediately to the up position, thus creating a down-up motion.

The stroke is executed from the wrist, not the arms. The arms will be most-often used for lateral motions. Later, the arms may be used in the stroke action for volume and accents.

The piston-stroke.

There is very little (if any) natural rebound with mallet instruments, so the motion is executed completely from the wrist. Don't push the stroke into the bar. Instead, think of pulling the sound out of the bar.

Start by working with each hand individually. Do the following exercises with one hand, then with the other hand, then alternating hands. Strive to make the sound produced by the right-hand and left-hand strokes exactly the same. Remember, use a relaxed wrist motion of about 6" to 8".

Preliminary Exercises

Note: R is for the right hand, and L is for the left hand.

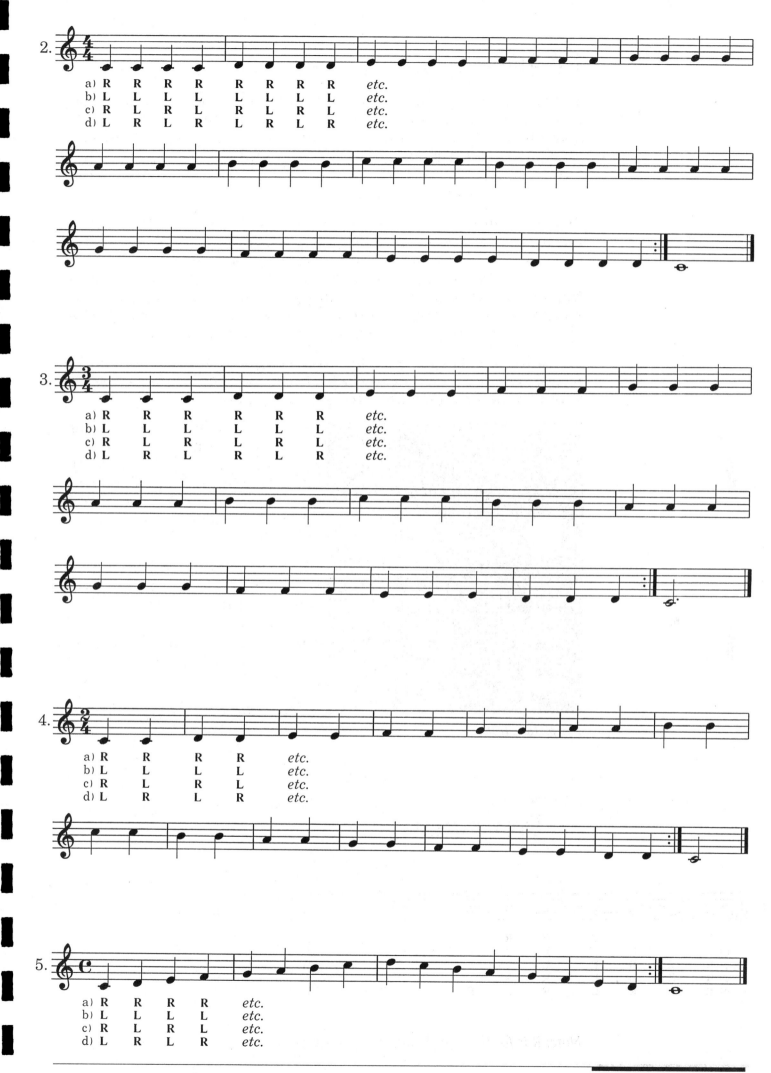

TECHNIQUE AND READING

The early studies in this book will be divided into two distinct areas: technique and reading. *The technique exercises are to be played from memory,* so that you can focus on proper execution and develop a feel for the keyboard.

Developing the ability to read on the mallet keyboard instruments is difficult and will take much patience. The player must develop a kinesthetic sense of intervallic relationships. The mallets have to travel through the air without any contact with the instrument and land on the right note. This challenge is multiplied by the fact that bar widths vary from instrument to instrument. Through practice and experience the player will learn to make adjustments that will enable him or her to play accurately on any kind or size of instrument.

The reading exercises are to be *read* at all times, even if you are able to play them without the music. In other words, keep your eyes on the music at all times. Early reading exercises tend to be easy to memorize, but in order to develop the ability to play accurately while reading music, it is important to avoid the temptation to look at the keyboard while playing these exercises. Don't get into the habit of looking at the music, then looking at the keyboard, then striking the bar, and then looking back at the music for the next note. Keep your eyes on the printed page and use your peripheral vision to judge where on the instrument you are playing.

Beginning mallet players tend to develop facility (technique) much faster than they develop the ability to read notes. The ultimate goal is to lessen the gap between technique and reading.

Try to read some new material every day. Music for flute, violin, oboe or almost any instrument can be used for sight-reading. Reading duets with another instrumentalist is also very helpful.

Ultimately, in actual performance (particularly of solos) one will probably want to play from memory; but the ability to read and play at the same time is very important and must be practiced conscientiously from the very beginning stages of study.

BEGINNING TECHNIQUE EXERCISES

The following exercises can be easily memorized, and should be played from memory. This will allow the freedom to focus on the hands and strokes, as well as to begin to develop a physical familiarity with the keyboard.

R. H. Alone

7.

L. H. Alone

8.

L R L R L R L R *etc.*

As new keys are introduced, the above patterns should be transposed and practiced in each new key.

READING

For the beginning student, the music stand should be placed in front of the instrument at the center. It should be about an inch above the sharp and flat bars, low enough so that you can see both the music and the bars. As the student becomes more comfortable with reading, it is a good idea to gradually increase the height of the music stand so that when playing in ensemble situations, the performer's line of vision will include both the music and the conductor.

When reading music, keep your eye on the music itself, and use your peripheral vision to find your way around the keyboard. Remember: even though you may know the music you are playing, continue to look at the music as you practice.

The following reading exercises are designed to help the beginning student become familiar with the keyboard.

Play each exercise: 1. right hand alone
                    2. left hand alone
                    3. with indicated sticking

Recite each note name as you play it.

Beginning Reading Studies

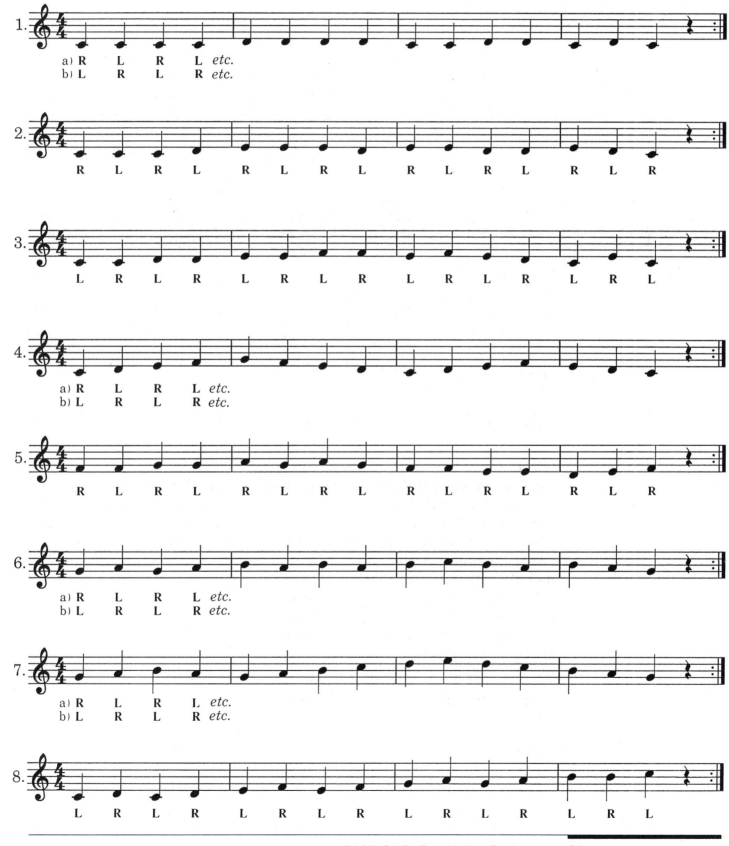

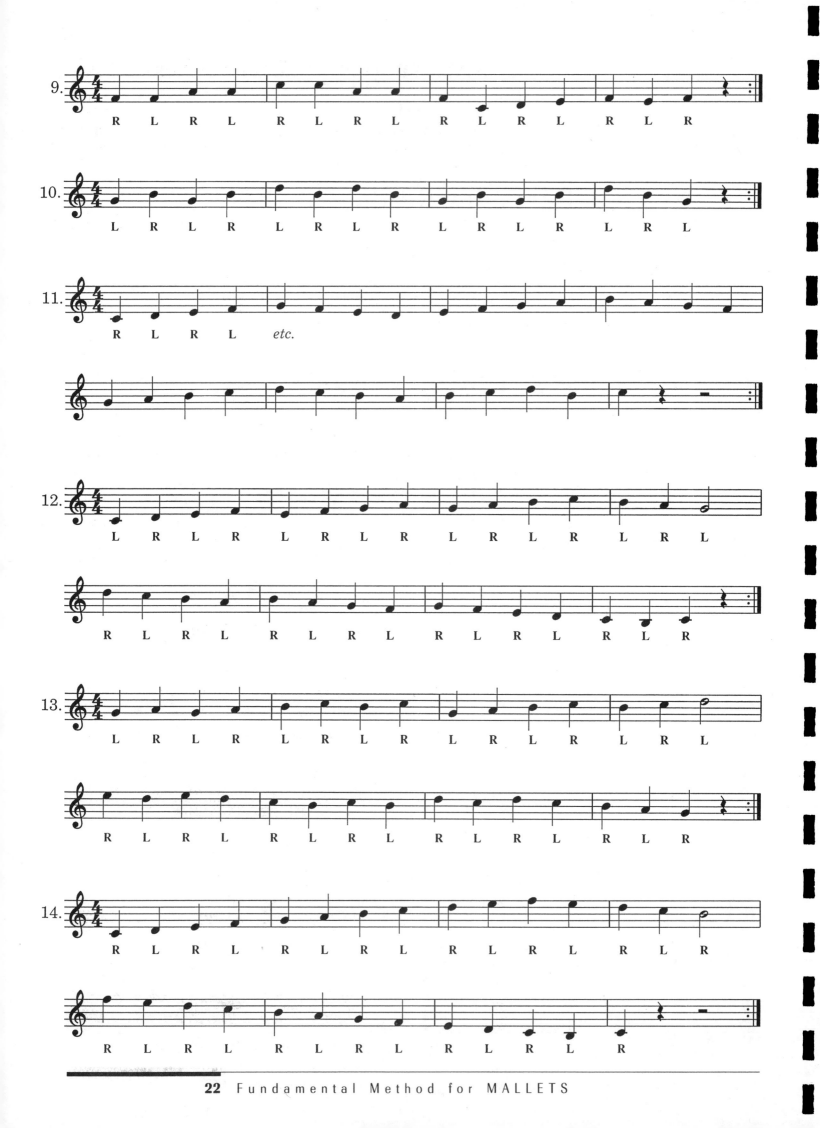

BASIC TECHNIQUE PATTERNS

The following technical patterns, based on the major scale and chord, are easily memorized and should be played from memory. Playing them from memory will allow you to focus more on: 1. hand position, 2. stroke motion, 3. evenness of sound between the right and left hands and 4. developing a familiarity with the keyboard. As new keys are introduced, the following patterns should be transposed and practiced in each new key. Additionally, these patterns are excellent for use as warm-up exercises.

C-Major Scale   C-Major Chord (Arpeggiated)

Play the following patterns from memory. Focus on relaxation, and evenness of tone between the right and left hands.

Repeat each pattern
many times.

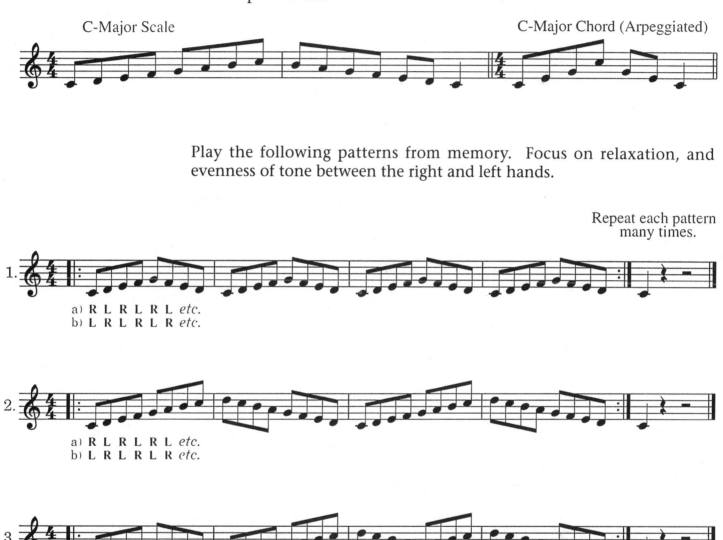

1.

a) **R L R L R L** *etc.*
b) **L R L R L R** *etc.*

2.

a) **R L R L R L** *etc.*
b) **L R L R L R** *etc.*

3.

a) **R L R L R L** *etc.*
b) **L R L R L R** *etc.*

4.

a) **R L R L R L** *etc.*
b) **L R L R L R** *etc.*

5.

a) **R L R L R L** *etc.*
b) **L R L R L R** *etc.*

6.

L R L R L R L R *etc.*

L R L R

R L R L R L R L *etc.*

R L R L   **R**

7.

a) **L R L R L R** *etc.*
b) **R L R L R L** *etc.*

8.

L R L R

L R L   **R L R L**

R L R

9.

R L R L *etc.*

R

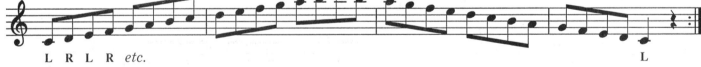

L R L R *etc.*

L

10.

L   **L**   **R**   **L**   **R**   **L**   **R**   **L**   **R**   **L**   **R**   **L**   **R**   **L**   **R**

11.

a) **R**   **L**   **R**   **L**   *etc.*
b) **L**   **R**   **L**   **R**   *etc.*

As each new key is learned, the above Basic Technique Patterns should be transposed and practiced in the new key.

The use of a metronome frequently (but not always) is highly recommended for the technical exercises. Speed and fluidity are goals with the technical exercises, but never at the expense of accuracy and evenness. Practicing an exercise rapidly but incorrectly is counterproductive.

Additionally, once the player has become comfortable with the notes, it is imperative to practice these exercises at various dynamic levels. One must develop the ability to play accurately at an extremely soft level as well as at louder levels.

STICKING

Basically, strokes on mallet instruments are alternated whenever possible and practical, though the doubling of strokes is often helpful and necessary in the execution of certain passages. Keep in mind that sticking choices will influence phrasing.

Sticking is ultimately a highly individual and personal decision. A few general points to consider in determining stickings are:

1. use hand-to-hand playing when possible or practical

2. when doubling is necessary, try to double between smaller intervals, rather than larger intervals

3. when possible, double between slower note values rather than quicker note values

4. try to avoid crossing the sticks, particularly with large intervals

5. avoid using three or four strokes in a row with the same hand.

THE ROLL

The roll is used to sustain the tone of the bar. It is achieved by playing a series of alternating, evenly matched, legato single strokes. It is used primarily on the xylophone and marimba, occasionally on the bells, and rarely on the vibraphone. The metal bars of the vibes and bells produce long sustaining sounds, and generally do not require rolls.

To start developing the roll, practice the following single-stroke patterns. Practice the patterns slowly at first, then gradually increase the speed and then slow down. Be sure to use a relaxed stroke and raise both mallets to the same height. As the speed of the single strokes increases, the strokes will become somewhat shorter.

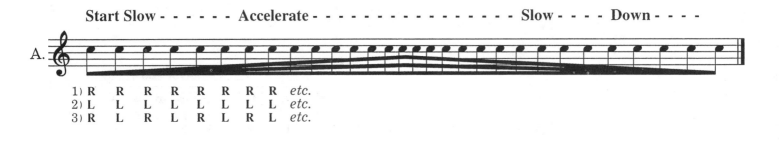

Start Slow - - - - - - Accelerate - - - - - - - - - - - - - - - - - Slow - - - - Down - - - -

A.

1) R   R   R   R   R   R   R   R   *etc.*
2) L   L   L   L   L   L   L   L   *etc.*
3) R   L   R   L   R   L   R   L   *etc.*

B.

1)	R	R	R	R	R	R	R	R	RLRLRLRL	RLRLRLRL
2)	L	L	L	L	L	L	L	L	LRLRLRLR	LRLRLRLR
3)	R	L	R	L	R	L	R	L	RLRLRLRL	RLRLRLRL
4)	L	R	L	R	L	R	L	R	LRLRLRLR	LRLRLRLR

Keep the left mallet in front of the right, except when rolling in the low register. When the mallets are to the far left of your body, reverse the position (place the right mallet in front of the left mallet).

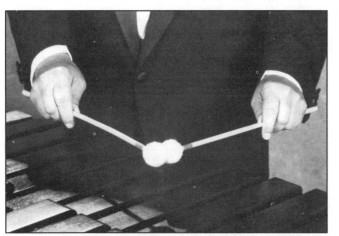

Rolling position, low register.

Rolling position, high register.

As the following patterns become comfortable, they should be played faster. These are exercises for developing the single stroke, which is the fundamental element from which the roll is produced. It should not be implied, however, that the roll is produced by playing a measured rhythm.

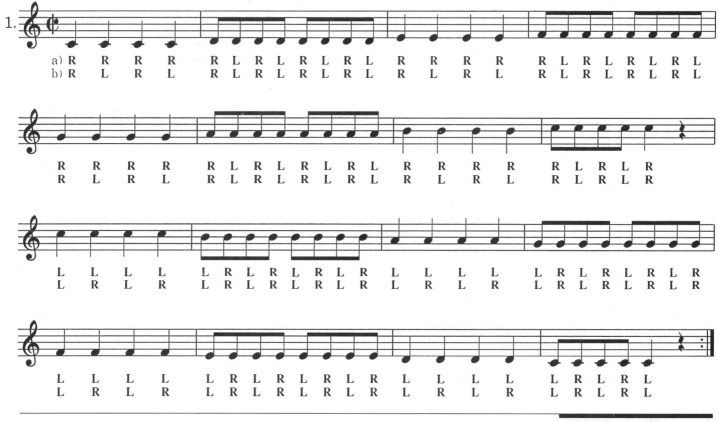

1.

a) R   R   R   R   RLRLRLRL   R   R   R   R   RLRLRLRL
b) R   L   R   L   RLRLRLRL   R   L   R   L   RLRLRLRL

R   R   R   R   RLRLRLRL   R   R   R   R   RLRLR
R   L   R   L   RLRLRLRL   R   L   R   L   RLRLR

L   L   L   L   LRLRLRLR   L   L   L   L   LRLRLRLR
L   R   L   R   LRLRLRLR   L   R   L   R   LRLRLRLR

L   L   L   L   LRLRLRLR   L   L   L   L   LRLRL
L   R   L   R   LRLRLRLR   L   R   L   R   LRLRL

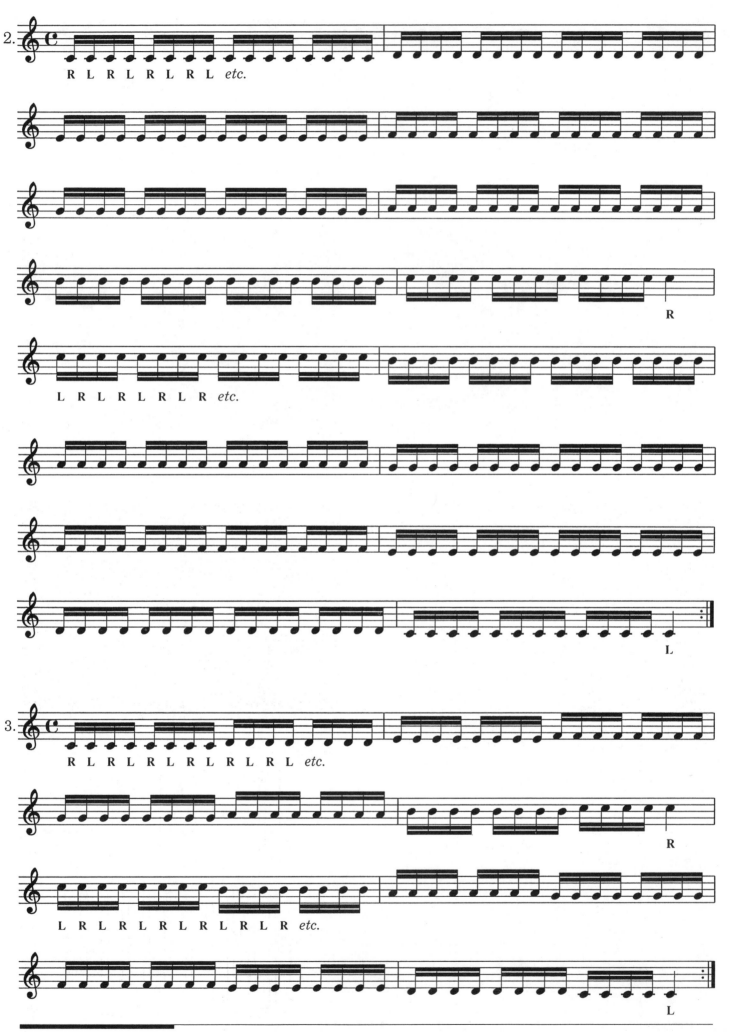

4. R L R L *etc.*

R

L R L R *etc.*

L

Work to achieve an even roll, rather than a fast roll. Speed will come naturally as the result of consistent practice.

Ultimately, the actual speed of the roll will vary depending on the pitch (high notes must be rolled faster), material of the bar (hard woods and certain synthetics demand a more rapid roll), volume (increased speed helps to reinforce increased volume) and expression (professional performers vary roll speed as a means of expression, much like a violinist's vibrato). If you don't roll fast enough, the tone will not sustain; if you roll too fast the tone will sound harsh and choked.

Rolls on the accidental bars may be played in two ways: 1. both mallets in the center of the bar and 2. one mallet in the center of the bar, the other mallet on the end of the bar.

Rolling on Accidental,
both mallets center.

Rolling on Accidental,
1 mallet center/ 1 mallet edge.

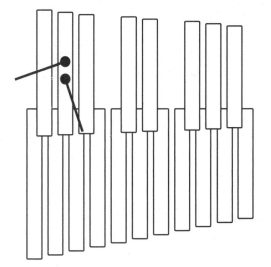

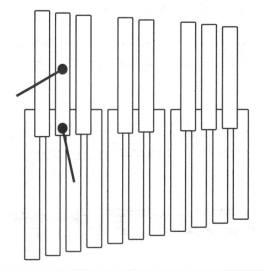

The roll for mallet instruments may be designated with the standard three slashes crossing the note's stem or with three slashes placed above a whole note. Some composers use *tr* (tremolo) to designate a roll.

(most common method)

Unless indicated as a roll, notes of long duration are not rolled, but are struck.

Play Exercises 1–4 twice as follows: 1. start rolls with right hand
2. start rolls with left hand

Beginning Roll Exercises

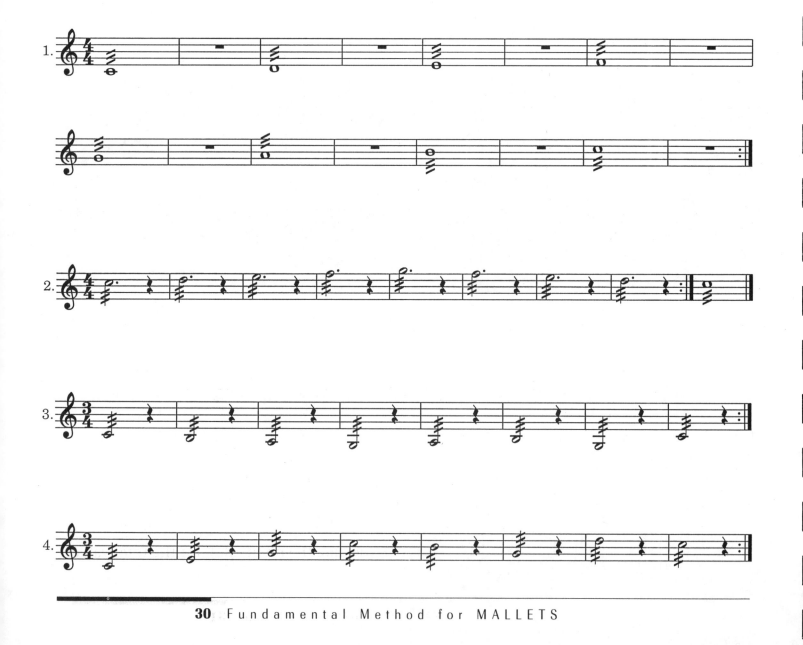

Practice the following exercises (5–13) detached (i.e. with a slight break between each note). As the player becomes more comfortable with the roll, the exercises should then be practiced legato (without any break or space between the notes), so that the sound is smooth and continuous. Legato rolls are indicated by means of a slur (⌒) connecting the notes. The sticking notated indicates the hand that begins the roll. The performer must be able to start rolls with either hand.

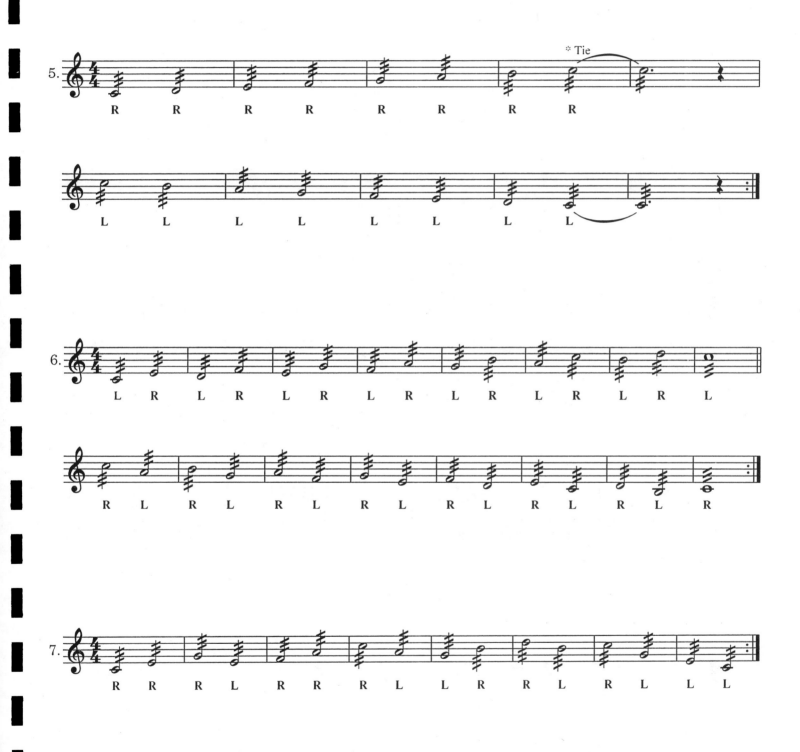

*When a tie occurs, do not rearticulate the pitch. Roll for the total value of both notes.

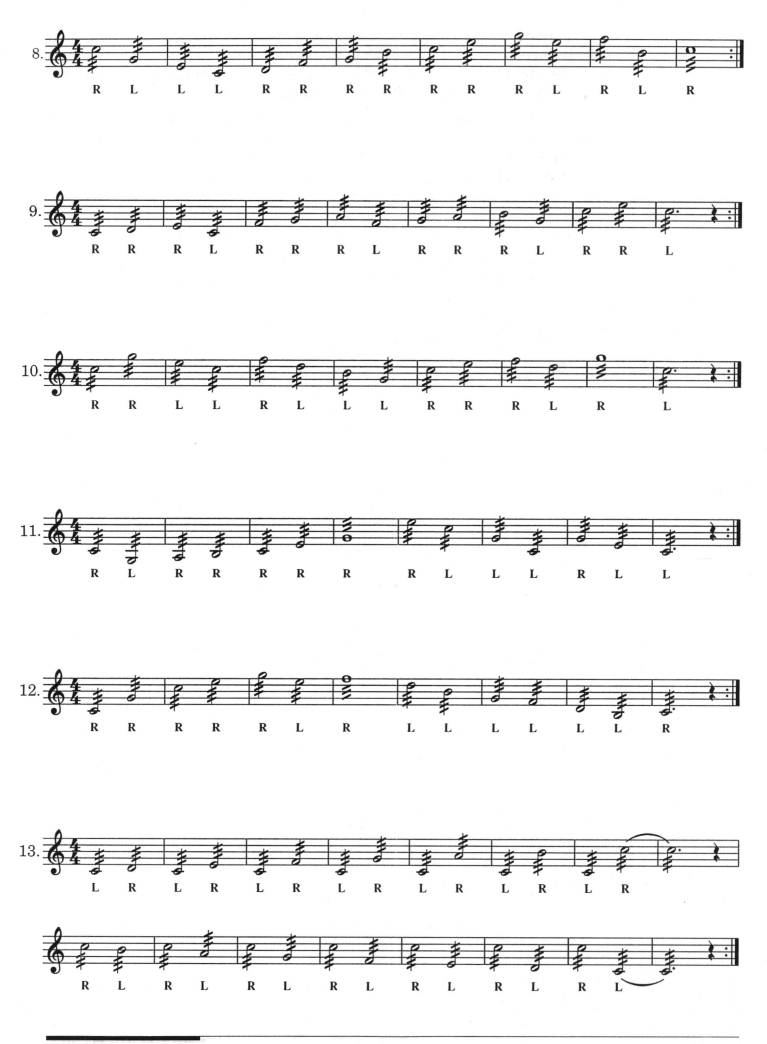

Playing legato or tied rolls requires a smooth, refined technique. The mallets must shift very quickly from one note to another without breaking the roll, so that it sounds continuous. The wider the interval, the more difficult it is to achieve the desired smoothness.

Practice so that you will be able to start rolls with either hand. Generally, when moving up or to the right, lead the move with the right hand; when moving down or to the left, lead the move with the left hand. When moving to an accidental bar from a natural bar, lead with the left hand; and when moving to a natural bar from an accidental bar, lead the move with the right hand. (This assumes that you are using the basic position of the left mallet being placed ahead of the right mallet.)

When a roll is preceded by a single stroke, the sticking should alternate into the roll. In other words, don't begin the roll with the same hand that played the preceding stroke.

When rolling legato on repeated notes of the same pitch, break the roll very slightly just before the repeated note to create rearticulation of the pitch. Be careful not to accent the repeated pitch.

Reading Studies

C Major

Remember, the Reading Studies are to be read, not memorized.

Technical Exercises

G Major

Play all Basic Technique Patterns from pages 23–25 in the key of G major.

Repeat each exercise
many times.

5.

Practice Exercise 6 at a very slow tempo.

1. Practice slightly detached, beginning all rolls with the right hand.

2. Practice slightly detached, beginning all rolls with the left hand.

3. Practice slightly detached, with the indicated sticking.

4. Practice legato (slurred), with the indicated sticking.

6.

Note: The technical exercises contain no tempo or dynamic indications. It is intended that the student practice them at all dynamic levels (loud, soft, crescendo, diminuendo), and at varied tempos.

7.

L   R   L   R   L   L   R   L   R   *etc.*

R   L   R   L   R   L   R   L   *etc.*

Remember, the Technical Exercises are to be played from memory so that you can concentrate on your hands.

Reading Studies

G Major

Technical Exercises

F Major

Play all Basic Technique Patterns from pages 23–25 in the key of F major.

Repeat each exercise
many times.

3.

a) R L R L R R L R L R *etc.*
b) L R L R L L R L R L *etc.*

4.

L L L L

L R R R R

R

5.
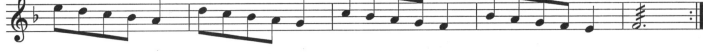

a) R L R L *etc.*
b) L R L R *etc.*

6.

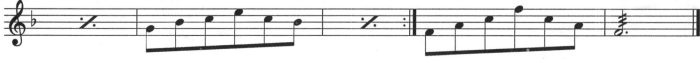

L R *etc.*

Reading Studies

F Major

Technical Exercises

D Major

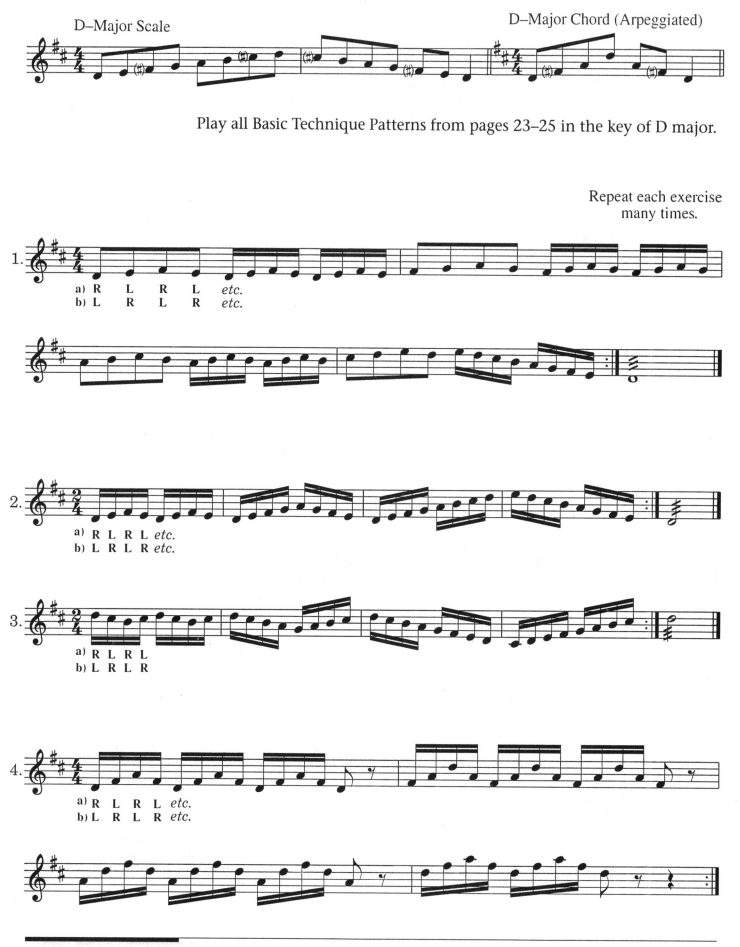

Play all Basic Technique Patterns from pages 23–25 in the key of D major.

Repeat each exercise
many times.

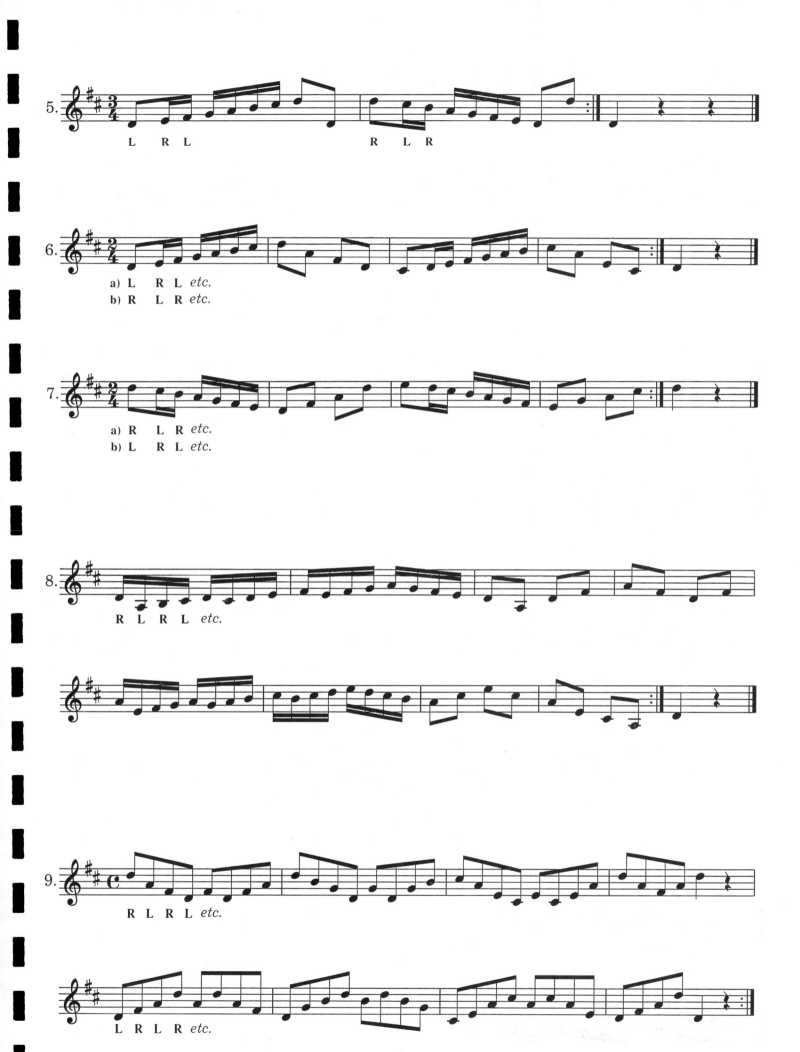

Remember, the Technical Exercises are to be played from memory so that you can concentrate on your hands.

Reading Studies

D Major

Remember, the Reading Studies are to be read, not memorized.

Technical Exercises

B♭ Major

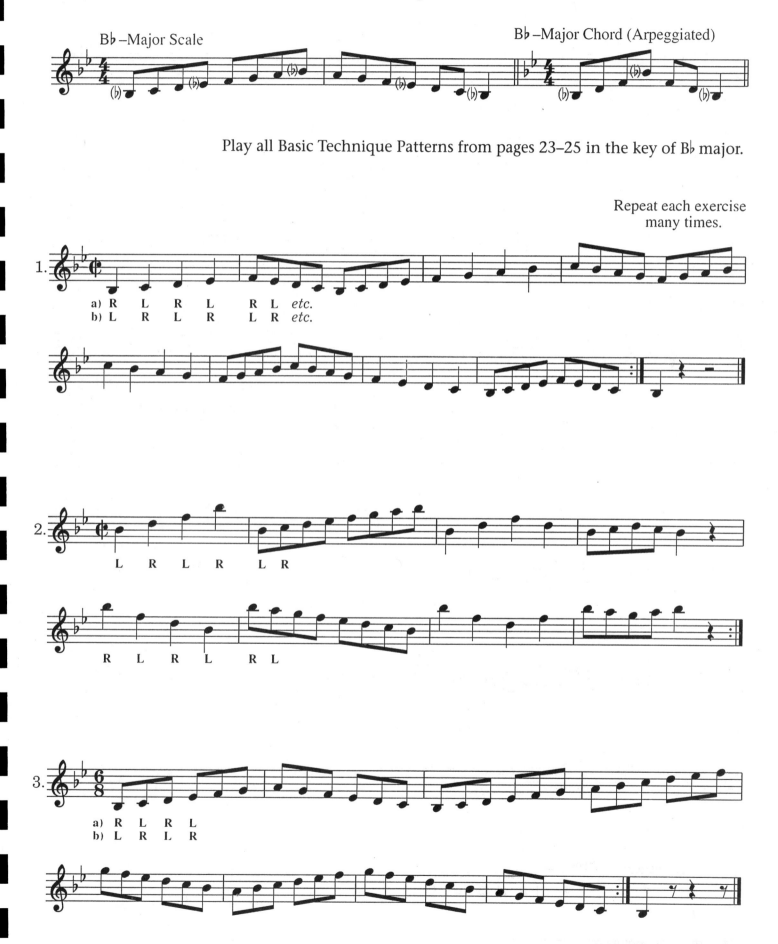

Play all Basic Technique Patterns from pages 23–25 in the key of B♭ major.

Repeat each exercise
many times.

Reading Studies

Bb Major

Technical Exercises

Chromatic Scale

Repeat each exercise
many times.

5.
a) R   L   R   L
b) L   R   L   R

6.
a) R   L   R   L
b) L   R   L   R

7.
a) R   L   R   L
b) L   R   L   R

8.
a) R   L   R   L
b) L   R   L   R

9.
a) R   L   R   L
b) L   R   L   R

a) R   L   R   L
b) L   R   L   R

10.

Transpose all of the above exercises (1–10) to begin on the various notes of the chromatic scale.

Reading Studies

Chromatic Scales

Allegro Moderato

1.

Moderato

2.

Allegro

3.

The major scale has only one form, but the minor scale has three different forms:

1. natural minor,
2. harmonic minor and
3. melodic minor.

The most common form is the harmonic minor. The mallet player should be acquainted with all three forms.

Technical Exercises
A Minor

A Natural Minor Scale

Relative Major Scale/C Major

A Harmonic Minor Scale (2 Octaves)

A Melodic Minor Scale (2 Octaves)

A Minor Chord (Arpeggiated)

Play all Basic Technique Patterns from pages 23–25 in the key of A minor, using both the harmonic and melodic forms of the scale.

Remember, the Technical Exercises are to be played from memory so that you can concentrate on your hands.

Reading Studies

A Minor

Moderato

3.

A thorough knowledge of the bass clef is necessary for the mallet player, particularly as one delves into the solo marimba repertoire. The following studies are presented to introduce the student to the notes of the bass clef. If one doesn't have a marimba available to practice these exercises as written, then play them up an octave or two on the available instrument.

Bass Clef Studies

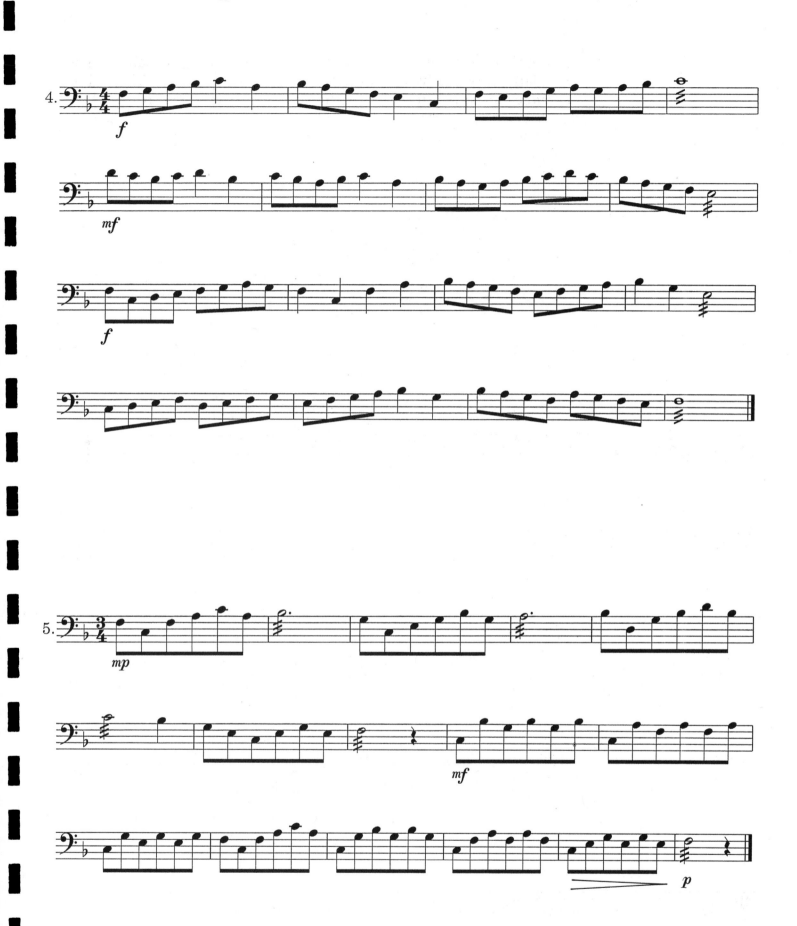

6.

7.

8.

Two notes played at the same time are referred to as double stops. Be sure both notes are struck *exactly at the same time.*

Technical Exercises

Double Stops

Repeat each exercise many times.

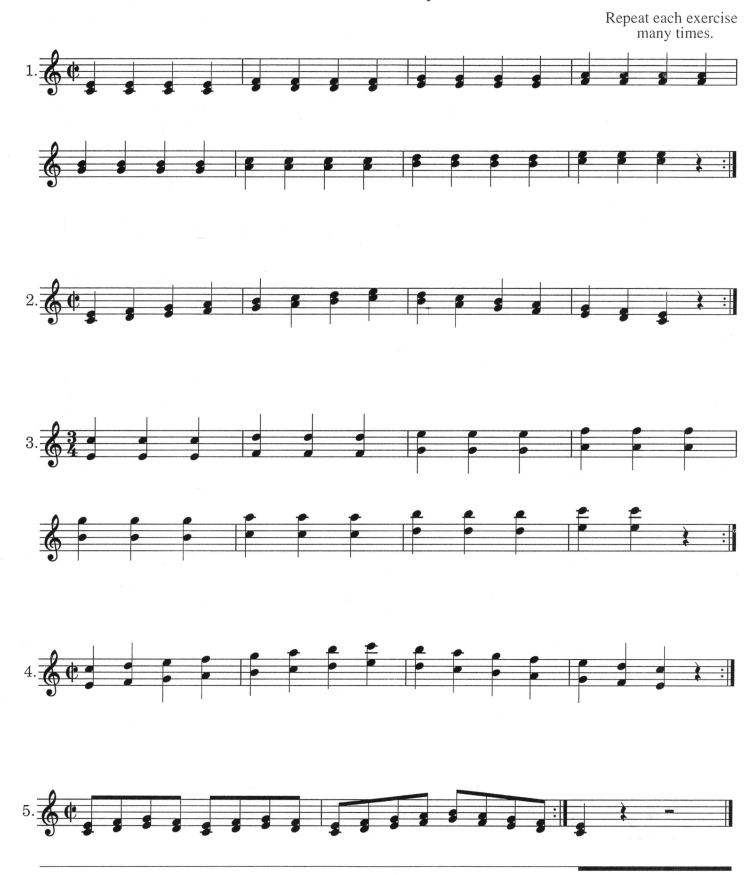

Reading Studies

Double Stops

Moderato

2.

mf

cresc.   *f*

mp

mf

f

Allegro

3.

f

p   *mp*   *mf*   *cresc.*

f

Technical Exercises

A Major

A–Major Scale

A–Major Chord (Arpeggiated)

Play all Basic Technique Patterns from pages 23–25 in the key of A major.

Repeat each exercise
many times.

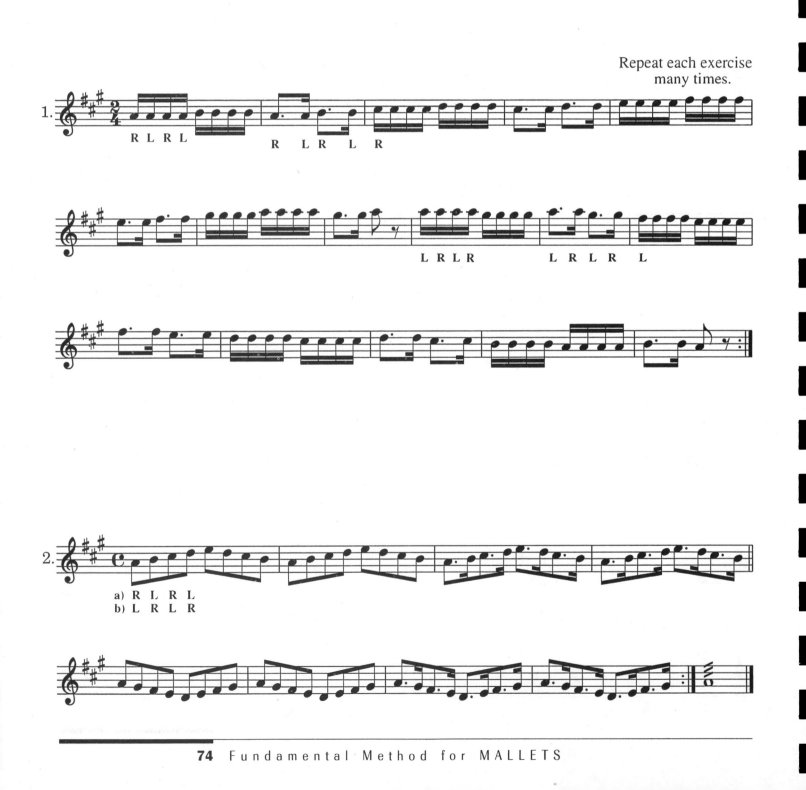

1.

R L R L   R L R L R

L R L R   L R L R L

2.

a) R L R L
b) L R L R

6.

7. L R L R

8. L R L R

R L R L

9. L R L R

R L R L

Reading Studies

A Major

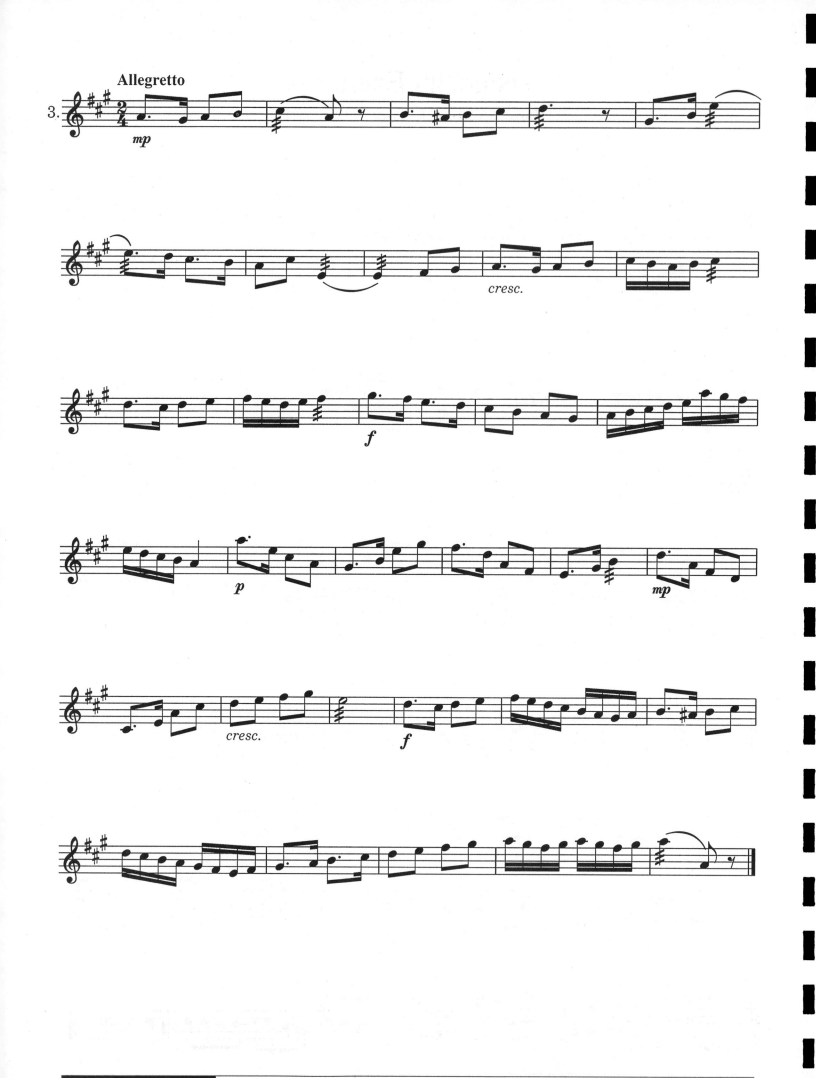

Technical Exercises
Double Strokes/Repeated Notes

Repeat each exercise
many times.

1.
a) **R L R L** *etc.*   **R R L L** *etc.*
b) **L R L R** *etc.*   **L L R R** *etc.*

2.
a) **R L R L** *etc.*
b) **R R L L** *etc.*
c) **L R L R** *etc.*
d) **L L R R** *etc.*

3.
R R L L R R L L   R R L L *etc.*

4.
L L R R L L R R   L L R R *etc.*

5.

R R L L R R L L *etc.*

L L R R L L R R *etc.*

6.

R R L L R R L L *etc.*

7.

L L R R L L R R *etc.*

8.

a) **R R L L L R R L L**
b) **L L R R L L L R R**

9.

L L R R L L L R R L L R R   L L R R

R R L L R R L L L R R L L

R R L L

Technical Exercises

E Minor

E–Natural Minor Scale

Relative–Major Scale/ G Major

E–Harmonic Minor Scale

E–Melodic Minor Scale

E–Minor Chord (Arpeggiated)

Play all Basic Technique Patterns from pages 23–25 in the key of E minor, using both the harmonic and melodic forms of the scale.

Repeat each exercise
many times.

(Harmonic Minor Scale)

1.

L R L R

(Melodic Minor Scale)

2.

R L R L

3.

4.

5.

Reading Studies

E Minor

Vivace

3.

f R L R L   R L L R L L R L L R L L   R L R L   R L L R L L

L R L R   L R R L R R   L R L R

Allegro non troppo

4.

p LL RR LL RR

RR LL RR LL   *cresc.*

mf

f

Technical Studies
E♭ Major

E♭ –Major Scale

E♭ –Major Chord (Arpeggiated)

Play all Basic Technique Patterns from pages 23–25 in the key of E♭ major.

Repeat each exercise
many times.

1.

a) L R L R L R *etc.*
b) R L R L R L *etc.*

2.

a) L R L R R L R L R R *etc.*
b) L L R L R L L R L R *etc.*

a) R L R L L L R L R L L
b) R R L R L R R L R L L

3.

L R   R R L   L L R   R R L   L

4.

5.

6.

L R L R   R   L R L R   R

R   R

RLRL

L   RLRL

7.

a) L   R
b) R   L

8.

a) R   L
b) L   R

9.

L R L R

Reading Studies

Eb Major

Andante

Technical Exercises
D Minor

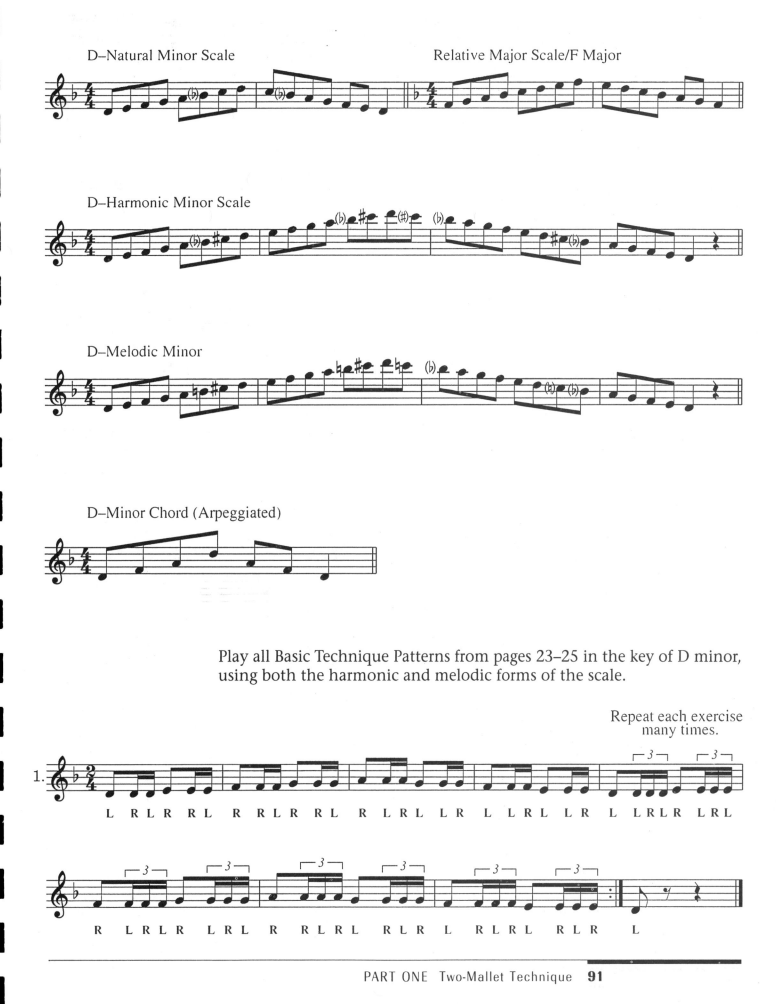

Play all Basic Technique Patterns from pages 23–25 in the key of D minor, using both the harmonic and melodic forms of the scale.

Repeat each exercise many times.

Reading Studies

D Minor

Allegro Moderato

Technical Exercises
E Major

E–Major Scale

E–Major Chord (Arpeggiated)

Play all Basic Technique Patterns from pages 23–25 in the key of E major.

Repeat each exercise
many times.

1.
a) R L
b) L R

2.
a) R L
b) L R

3.

4.

Reading Studies

E Major

Technical Exercises
G Minor

G–Natural Minor Scale   Relative–Major Scale/B♭ Major

G–Harmonic Minor Scale

G–Melodic Minor Scale

G–Minor Chord (Arpeggiated)

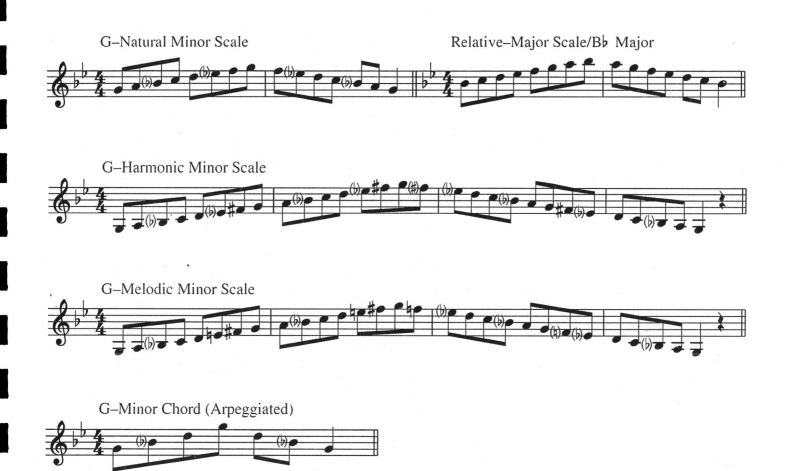

Play all Basic Technique Patterns from pages 23–25 in the key of G minor, using both the harmonic and melodic forms of the scale.

Repeat each exercise
many times.

1.

    a) R L R L
    b) L R L R

2.

    a) R L R L
    b) L R L R

3. a) R L R L
   b) L R L R

4. a) R R R L R R R L
   b) R L R L R L R L

a) L L L R L L L R
b) L R L R L R L R

5. L R L R L R L R

R L R L R L R L R L

6. a) R L R L
   b) L R L R

7.

L R L R

R L R L

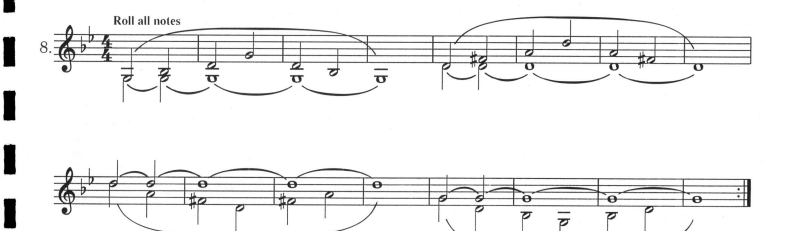

8. Roll all notes

Reading Studies

G Minor

Allegro

Technical Exercises
A♭ Major

Play all Basic Technique Patterns from pages 23–25 in the key of A♭ major.

Reading Studies

A♭ Major

poco rit.

Moderato
(in 2)

3.

Technical Exercises

B Minor

B-Natural Minor Scale

Relative-Major Scale/D Major

B-Harmonic Minor Scale

B-Melodic Minor Scale

B-Minor Chord (Arpeggiated)

Play all Basic Technique Patterns from pages 23–25 in the key of B minor, using both the harmonic and melodic forms of the scale.

Repeat each exercise many times.

1. R R L R L R L

2. L L R L R L R

3.

8.

9.

10.

Reading Studies

B Minor

1. **Slowly & Leisurely**

mp

mf

dim.

f

dim.

Moderato

2.

Andantino

3.

One should begin practicing four-mallet technique (playing with two mallets in each hand) early in the study of mallet technique. Ideally, as soon as the student has developed a fair degree of facility with two-mallet technique, he or she should begin acquiring four-mallet technique.

Playing with two mallets and playing with four mallets have almost nothing technically and physically in common.

FOUR-MALLET GRIPS

There are a number of different ways to hold four mallets. The three most common in use today tend to be referred to as the Musser-Stevens grip, the Burton grip, and the traditional cross-grip.

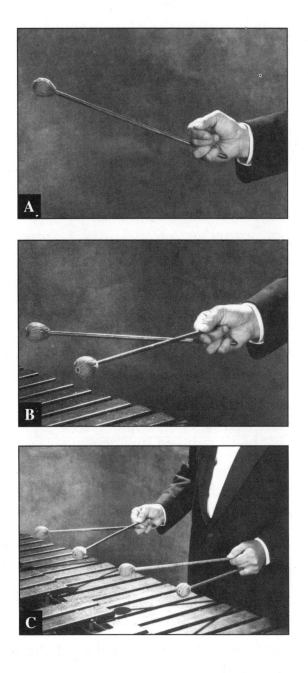

A.

B.

C.

MUSSER-STEVENS GRIP

The Musser-Stevens grip is preferred by most classically oriented marimbists. For the mallet performer dealing with marimba solo literature, this grip offers the most potential. The grip was invented by Clair Omar Musser, a famous marimba teacher, composer and performer of the 1930s. Leigh Howard Stevens revised the original grip a great deal, and it is this form of the grip that is most common today. The advantages of the modified grip are: 1) it allows the greatest independence between the two mallets in one hand, 2) it allows for the largest intervallic reaches and the smallest reaches (major and minor 2nds) with ease and comfort, and 3) it allows for the most flexibility with which to execute various types of rolls.

With the palm facing the wall, place the end of the outer mallet between the middle and ring fingers. The ring and little fingers should curl around the stick, holding it near the very end. (See photo A.) Place the inner mallet so that it is resting on the first joint of the index finger, with the bottom portion of the thumb resting on the stick. The butt end of the mallet will be in contact with the inside of the palm of the hand. (See photo B.) The thumb and index finger will control the inside mallet, and the fourth and fifth fingers will control the outside mallet. The mallets are held the same in both hands. (See photo C.)

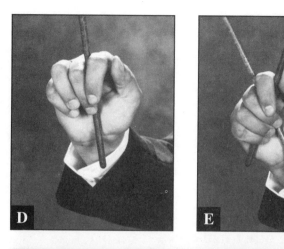

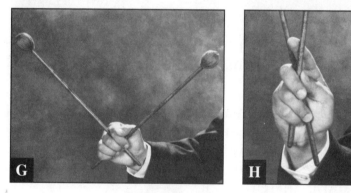

BURTON GRIP

This grip is very popular with vibe players, as well as most performers of jazz and rock. Developed by vibraphonist Gary Burton, it is a variation of the old-fashioned cross-grip.

The basic or starting mallet position is the same in both hands. Place the outer mallet between the index finger and middle finger, next to the palm. (See photo D.) The middle finger and sometimes the fourth finger (depending on the size of the player's hands) are used to anchor this mallet in place. This mallet stays stationary at all times, including when opening and closing the mallets. Next, cross the inner mallet over the other, holding it between the thumb and index finger while the other fingers curl around it. (See photo E.) The thumb rests outside of the inner mallet. In the basic or starting position, the mallets are spread at about a 45 degree angle. The inside mallet will extend out past the outside mallet about the length of a mallet head. (See photo F.)

The mallets are spread by sliding the index finger down between the mallets as the thumb starts to come over the inside mallet (the mallet that crosses over the stationary mallet), and at the same time, by pulling the end of the shaft of the inside mallet up with the fourth and fifth fingers. With wide intervals, the thumb will be completely inside and over the shaft of the inner mallet. (See photo G.) The fourth and fifth fingers play a very important role in opening and closing the mallets, by pulling or pushing the inner mallet in conjunction with the motion of the thumb and index finger.

The mallets are closed by moving the thumb back to the outside of the shaft and pushing the mallets together as the index finger moves back to its basic position; at the same time, push the mallet shaft back to its basic position with the fourth and fifth fingers. Close intervals are obtained by pointing the index finger between the mallet shafts and allowing the middle-finger anchor to move away from the palm in order to facilitate the move of the thumb and index finger. The fourth finger may assist in the anchoring of the outside mallet's shaft on close intervals. (See photo H.)

Single-line melodies are often played with the inside mallet of the left hand and the outside mallet of the right hand.

TRADITIONAL CROSS-GRIP

With this grip the inner mallets are held as with the normal two-mallet grip, and the outside mallets are added between the index and middle finger.

Place the inner mallet between the index finger and thumb as with the two-mallet grip, then place the outer mallet between the index finger and the middle finger, with the back part of the mallet crossing over the other mallet. Wrap, or curl, the last three fingers around the crossed shafts of the mallets, griping the mallets firmly with the last two fingers. (See photo I.)

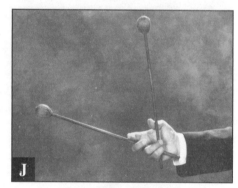

To spread the mallets, insert the thumb toward the inside of the first mallet, and spread the thumb and index finger apart, thus causing the mallets to spread apart. (See photo J.) To close the mallets, move the thumb back to the outside of the first mallet, and in conjunction with the three back fingers, squeeze the shafts together. To obtain the close interval of a second, it is necessary to point the index finger straight forward between the shafts. (See photo K.)

This grip was the original four-mallet grip, and is probably the easiest to learn, but it has the least technical potential and the most problems of the four-mallet grips, and is therefore not recommended.

Playing Position for Traditional Cross-Grip

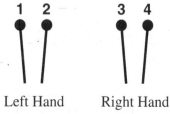

Left Hand   Right Hand

IDENTIFICATION OF MALLETS

For the purpose of indicating stickings, the mallets are numbered from 1 to 4, from the player's left to his or her right. (Some composers and performers reverse the numbering procedure.)

DOUBLE VERTICAL STROKES

Once the grip has become fairly comfortable, the best technical starting point is the playing of two notes at the same time with one hand. The interval of a fifth is physically a comfortable interval.

The student should become comfortable with the use of two mallets in each hand before trying to play with both hands, or with all four mallets. Even after the student has combined the use of the two hands, working with each hand individually is still necessary and helpful.

Practice the following slowly, first with the right hand alone, then with the left hand alone, and finally with both hands at the same time, playing one octave apart.

As the above exercise becomes more comfortable, reduce the number of repetitions to three, then two, and finally, one. Use the above procedure in practicing the following patterns as well.

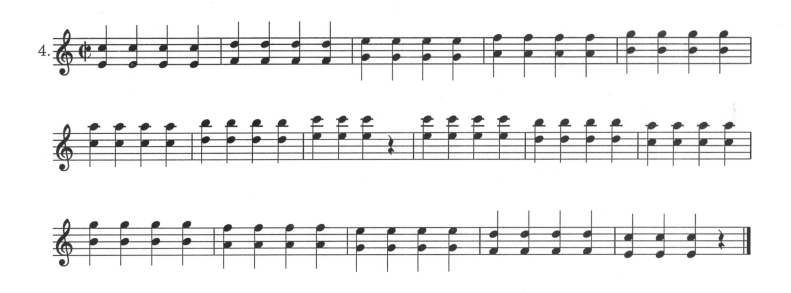

ROLLS

There are numerous types of rolls possible with multiple mallet grips. The most common roll and the one recommended for use in the early stage of studies and etudes in this volume is the traditional alternated stroke roll (double vertical stroke roll). In this roll both mallets in one hand strike the bars simultaneously, followed by both mallets in the other hand striking the bars simultaneously, etc.

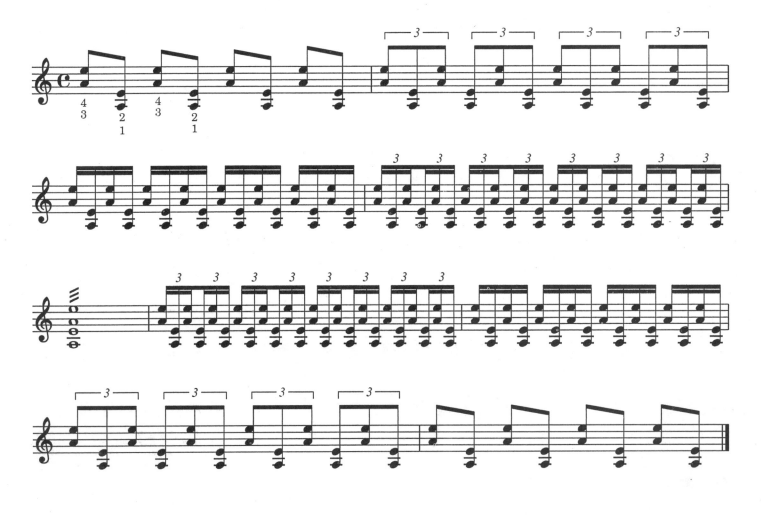

1. Roll all notes

Use the above pattern with parallel 4ths, 5ths and 6ths. As the rolls become comfortable, change the note values to half-notes, then quarter notes.

2.

Roll all notes

3.

Other rolls to be discussed later are as follows:

1. The "ripple" roll, where each mallet strikes the keyboard at a different time. This is achieved by holding the outside mallets firmly while the inside mallets pivot around a very loose fulcrum, causing the inside mallets to strike after the outside mallets when the strokes are alternated.

2. The "independent" roll, a technique developed by Leigh Stevens, in which each mallet strikes the keyboard independently. The effect is similar to the ripple roll, but the stroke of each mallet is controlled by the performer.

3. The "one-handed" roll, a roll executed with one hand, where the inside and outside mallets alternate by means of a rotary wrist motion.

Double-Vertical Strokes/Parallel Motion

Practice each hand alone, then together (in octaves).

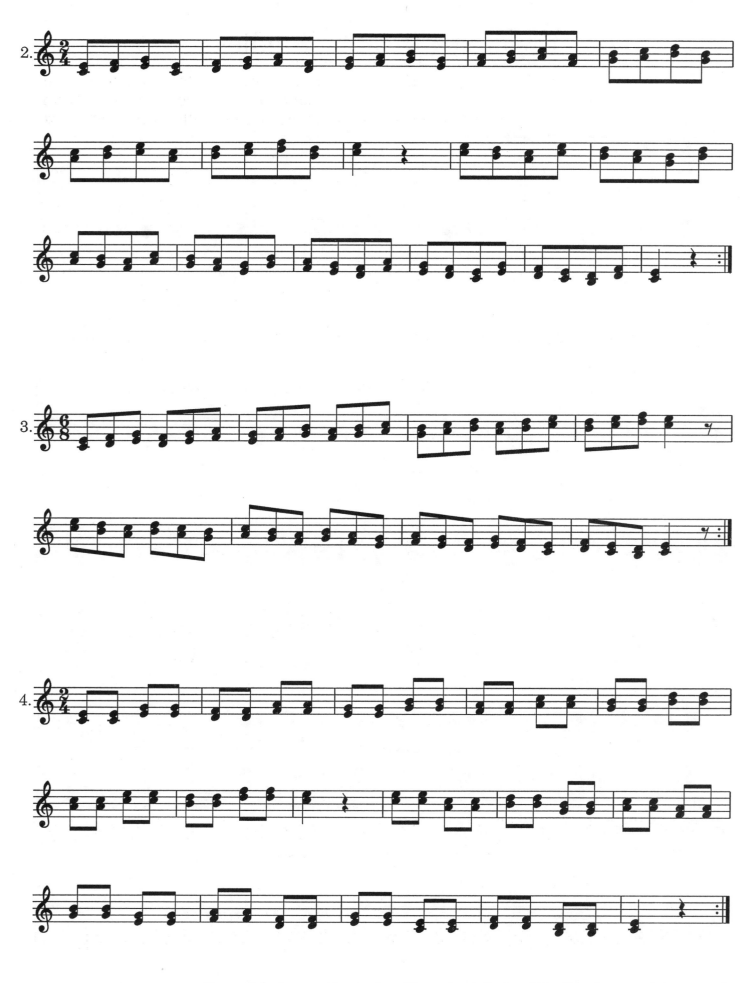

For added practice, play Exercises 1–4 with the interval inverted (parallel sixths).

Beginning Reading Studies

Double-Vertical Strokes/Spreading Exercises

Practice the following, first with the right hand alone, then with the left hand alone, and then with both hands at the same time playing an octave apart.

Spreading Exercises (Continued)

Developing Control of Changing Intervals

Practice first with the right hand alone, then with the left hand alone, then with both hands together, playing one octave apart.

11.

12.

13.

14.

15.

16.

17.

18.

19.

20.

21.

22.

23.

24.

Elementary Wrist Turns
(Chromatic Major 3rds)

Practice each hand separately, then hands together one octave apart.

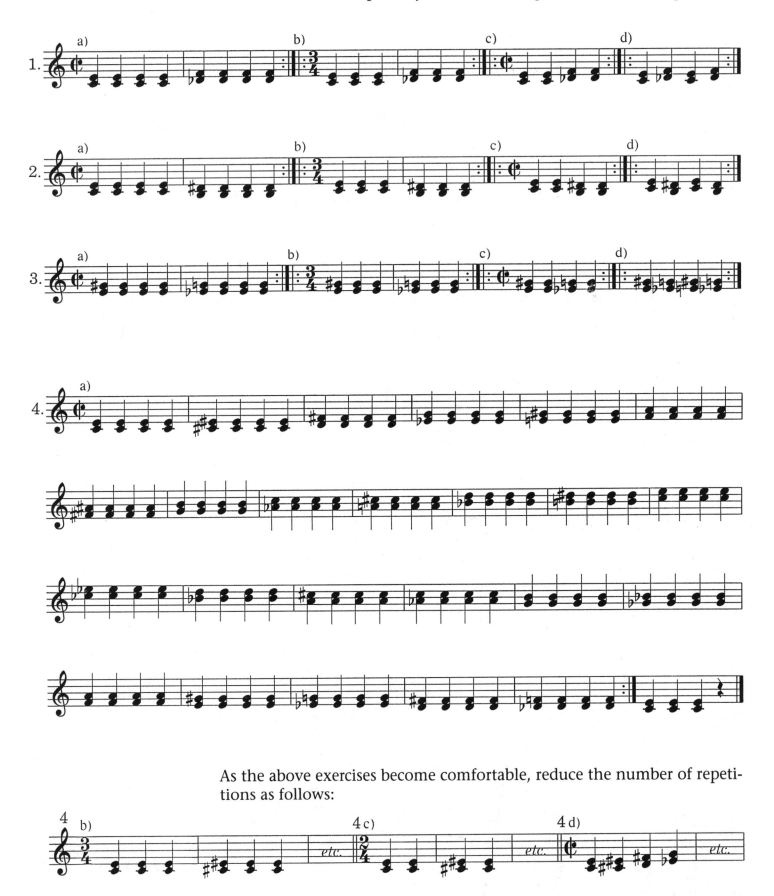

As the above exercises become comfortable, reduce the number of repetitions as follows:

Elementary Wrist Turns
(Chromatic Minor 3rds)

Practice each hand separately, then hands together one octave apart.

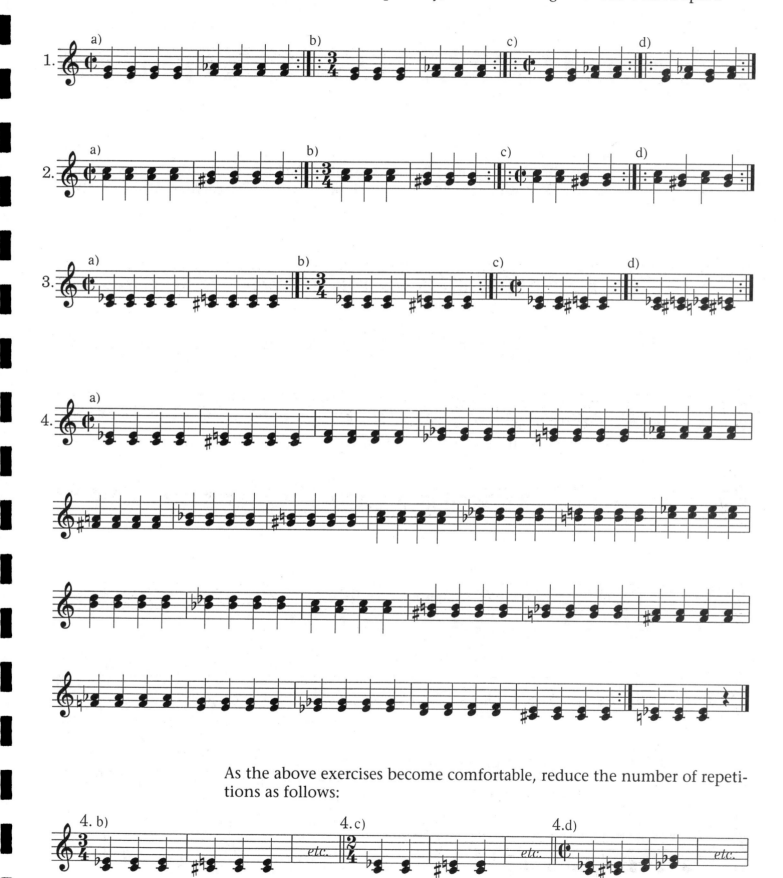

As the above exercises become comfortable, reduce the number of repetitions as follows:

Major Chords/4 Mallets

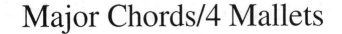

As the above exercise becomes comfortable, reduce the repetitions of each chord; first play each chord three times, then play each chord twice, then only once.

Practice the above exercise first separated, then legato or slurred.

The above exercises should be practiced with all major chords.

Major Chords/Chromatic Progression

As the above exercise becomes comfortable, reduce the repetitions of each chord. (Play each chord three times, then twice, then only once.)

Using the above chromatic sequence, practice the chords in different positions and voicings.

Var. I/1st Inversion – Closed Position

Continue

Chromatically

Var. II/2nd Inversion – Closed Position

Continue
Chromatically

Var. III/Root Position/Open Position

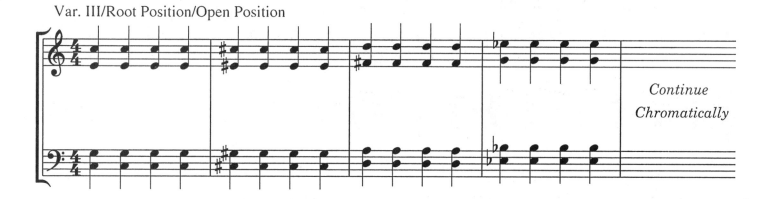

Continue
Chromatically

Var. IV/1st Inversion/Open Position

Continue
Chromatically

Var. V/2nd Inversion/Open Position

Continue
Chromatically

Minor Chords/4 Mallets

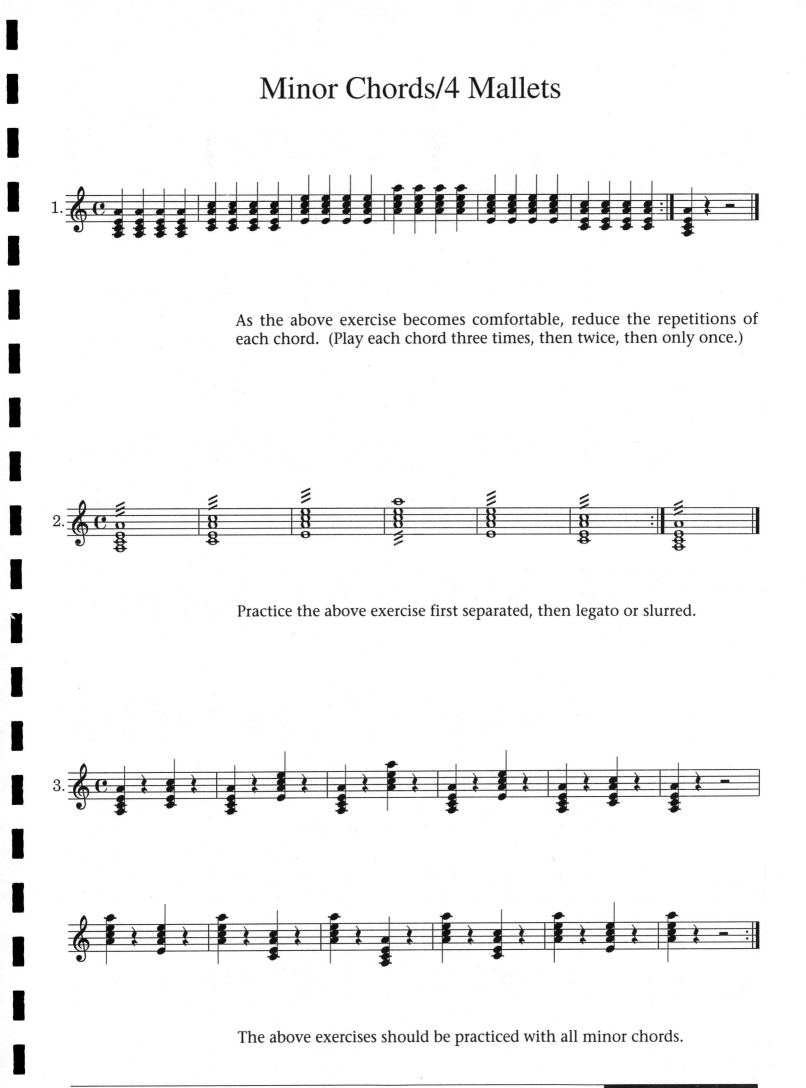

As the above exercise becomes comfortable, reduce the repetitions of each chord. (Play each chord three times, then twice, then only once.)

Practice the above exercise first separated, then legato or slurred.

The above exercises should be practiced with all minor chords.

Minor Chords/Chromatic Progression

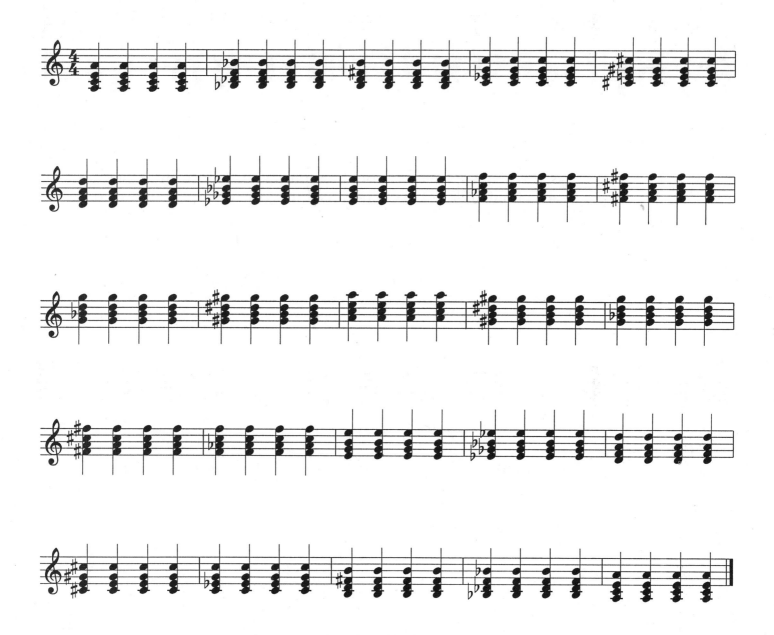

As the above exercise becomes comfortable, reduce the repetitions of each chord. (Play each chord three times, then twice, then only once.)

Using the above chromatic sequence, practice the chords in different positions and voicings.

Var. I/1st Inversion – Closed Position

Continue

Chromatically

Var. II 2nd Inversion/Closed Position

Continue

Chromatically

Var. III Root Position/Open Position

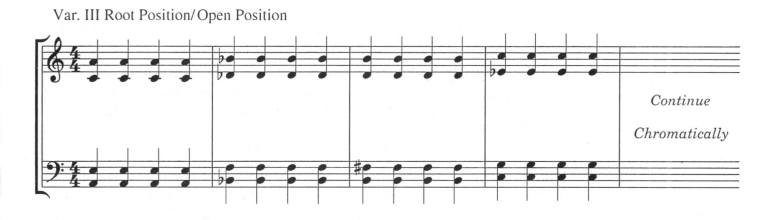

Continue

Chromatically

Var. IV 1st Inversion/Open Position

Continue

Chromatically

Var. V 2nd Inversion/Open Position

Continue

Chromatically

SINGLE INDEPENDENT STROKES

Four-mallet technique requires the development of a rotary wrist motion as well as the up and down motion that is the basis for two-mallet technique. The rotary wrist motion is similar to the motion used to turn a screwdriver.

The development of single independent strokes (the use of one mallet to strike a single note while gripping two mallets in the same hand) requires the use of this rotary motion. The goal is to strike the single stroke while keeping the unused mallet in the same hand as motionless as possible.

From a height of about 3 to 4 inches above the instrument, strike the bar with the single mallet, then return it to the original position above the instrument for the next stroke. The unused mallet should be low, close to the instrument, and should remain almost motionless. This motion must be developed with each of the four mallets.

The wrist motion used to play a rotary or single independent stroke with mallets 1 and 3 is like unscrewing a light bulb or jar top, while the motion for mallets 2 and 4 is like tightening a light bulb or a jar top.

When playing single-note lines, the two inside mallets are generally used.

Preliminary Exercises

Practice the following exercises with each mallet separately, keeping the unused mallet low and stationary. Use a rotating motion in the wrist.

1. Inside mallet, right hand (3)
2. Outside mallet, right hand (4)
3. Inside mallet, left hand (2)
4. Outside mallet, left hand (1)

1 2   3 4

Left Hand   Right Hand

1. Practice Exercise C with the inside mallet, right hand (3).

2. Practice Exercise C with the outside mallet, left hand (1), one octave lower.

3. Practice Exercise C with both hands together in octaves (1 and 3).

1. Practice Exercise D with the outside mallet, right hand (4).

2. Practice Exercise D with the inside mallet, left hand (2), one octave lower.

3. Practice Exercise D with both hands together in octaves (2 and 4).

Single Independent Stroke Exercises

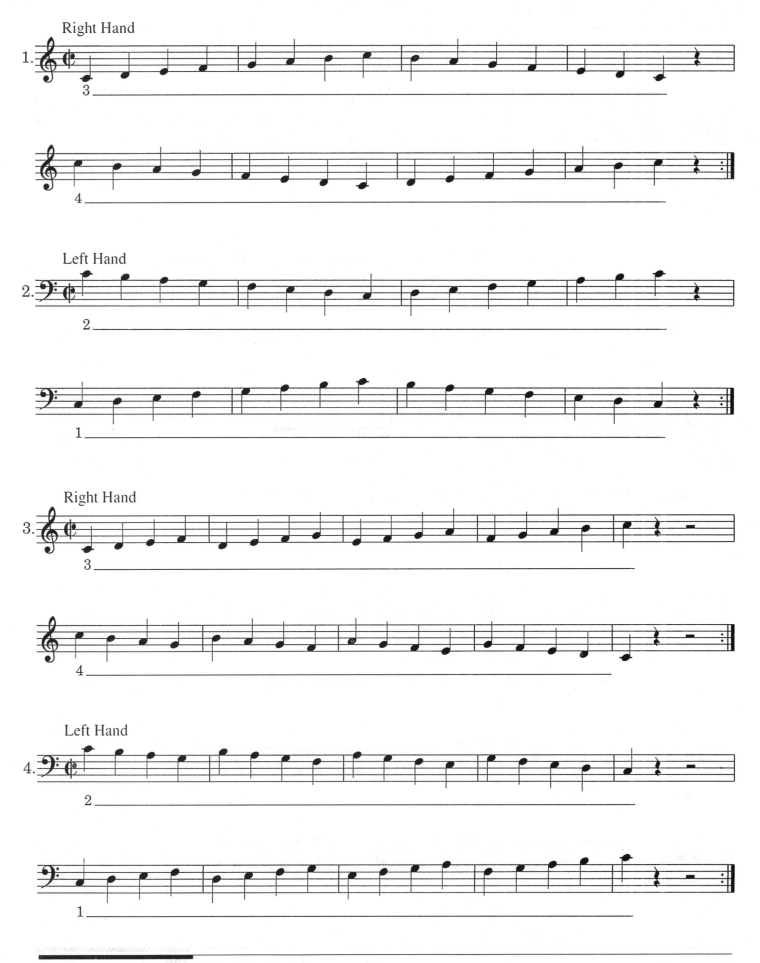

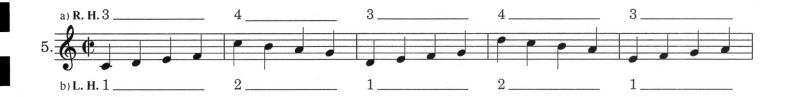

Single Independent Strokes
Combining Right and Left Hands

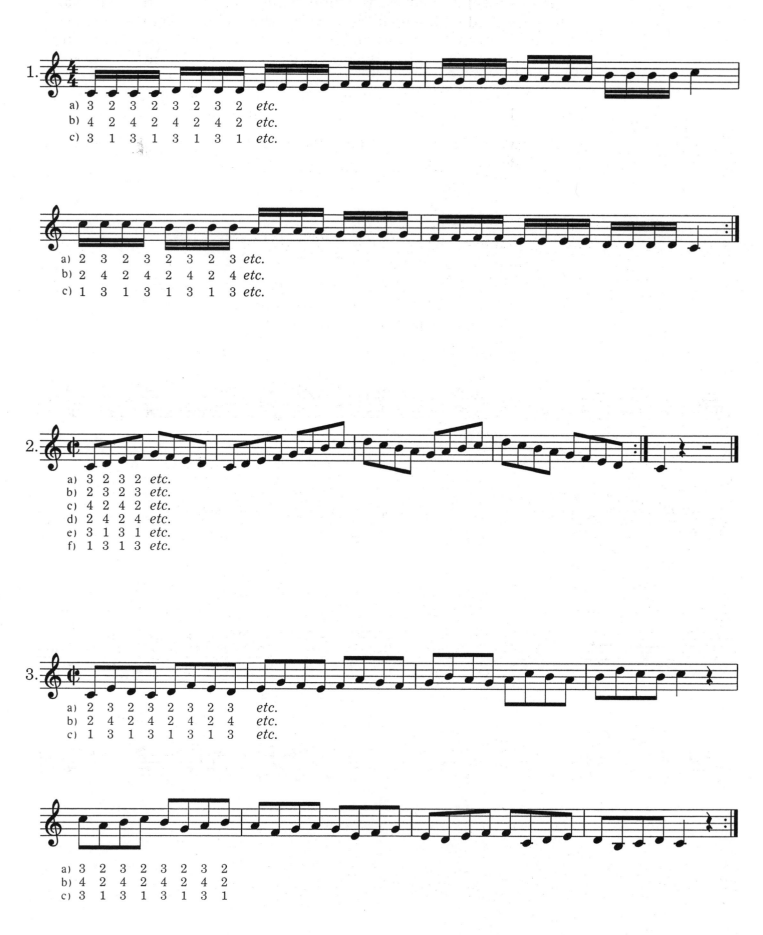

1.
a) 3 2 3 2 3 2 3 2 *etc.*
b) 4 2 4 2 4 2 4 2 *etc.*
c) 3 1 3 1 3 1 3 1 *etc.*

a) 2 3 2 3 2 3 2 3 *etc.*
b) 2 4 2 4 2 4 2 4 *etc.*
c) 1 3 1 3 1 3 1 3 *etc.*

2.
a) 3 2 3 2 *etc.*
b) 2 3 2 3 *etc.*
c) 4 2 4 2 *etc.*
d) 2 4 2 4 *etc.*
e) 3 1 3 1 *etc.*
f) 1 3 1 3 *etc.*

3.
a) 2 3 2 3 2 3 2 3 *etc.*
b) 2 4 2 4 2 4 2 4 *etc.*
c) 1 3 1 3 1 3 1 3 *etc.*

a) 3 2 3 2 3 2 3 2
b) 4 2 4 2 4 2 4 2
c) 3 1 3 1 3 1 3 1

SINGLE ALTERNATING STROKES

The single alternating stroke (referred to by some as the dependent rotary stroke) is an alternation of two pitches played by the same hand. It is executed with a rotary motion by which one mallet strikes one bar as the other mallet comes up off the instrument in preparation to strike another bar. That is, the downward motion of the first mallet raises the second mallet to its proper height, and as the second mallet descends, the first mallet is automatically raised to its proper starting height. Be particularly careful to produce the same volume with each mallet.

This technique serves as a preliminary motion for the development of the one-handed roll.

Practice the following:

1. right hand alone

2. left hand alone

3. both hands together, an octave apart

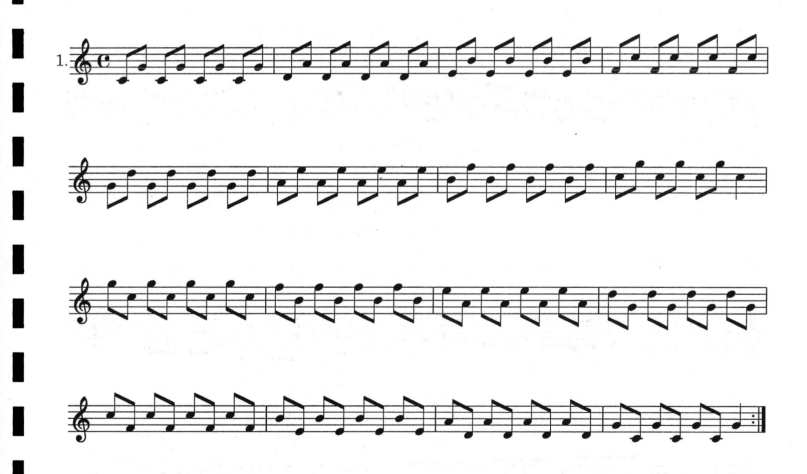

Using the diatonic pattern on the previous page as a guide, practice single alternating strokes with various intervals.

Var. I (4ths)

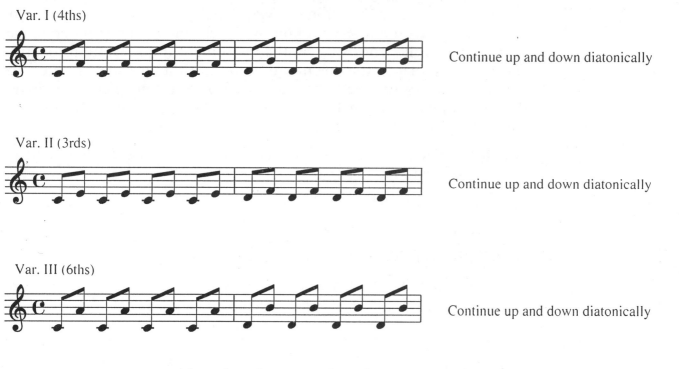

Continue up and down diatonically

Var. II (3rds)

Continue up and down diatonically

Var. III (6ths)

Continue up and down diatonically

After the above motions become comfortable, transpose the patterns into other keys.

7.

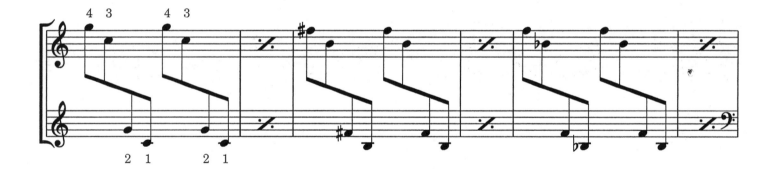

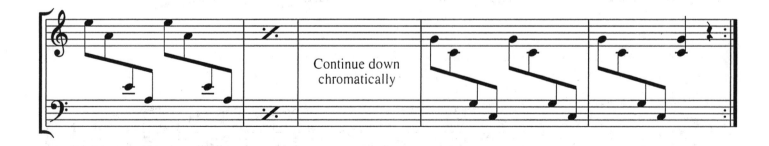

8.

Using the diatonic pattern on the previous page as a guide, practice with the following sticking variations.

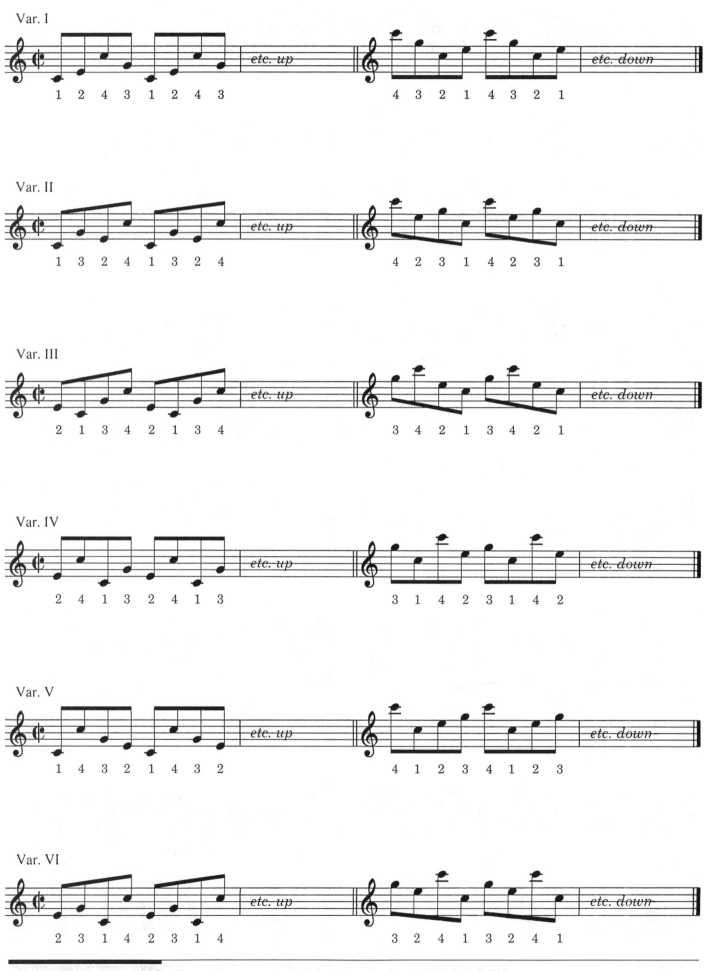

Var. I

1 2 4 3 1 2 4 3   *etc. up*   4 3 2 1 4 3 2 1   *etc. down*

Var. II

1 3 2 4 1 3 2 4   *etc. up*   4 2 3 1 4 2 3 1   *etc. down*

Var. III

2 1 3 4 2 1 3 4   *etc. up*   3 4 2 1 3 4 2 1   *etc. down*

Var. IV

2 4 1 3 2 4 1 3   *etc. up*   3 1 4 2 3 1 4 2   *etc. down*

Var. V

1 4 3 2 1 4 3 2   *etc. up*   4 1 2 3 4 1 2 3   *etc. down*

Var. VI

2 3 1 4 2 3 1 4   *etc. up*   3 2 4 1 3 2 4 1   *etc. down*

Elementary Chord Reading/Three Mallets

1. Practice with two mallets in the left hand and one in the right hand.
2. Practice with two mallets in the right hand and one in the left hand.

Elementary Chord Reading/Four Mallets

STUDIES

Play Study 1 with two mallets in the left hand and one in the right hand, then reverse; play with two mallets in the right hand and one in the left hand.

Play first by striking each chord once only. Next, play by rolling all chords.

Study No. 1

Study No. 2

Soldier's March

L. Streabbog

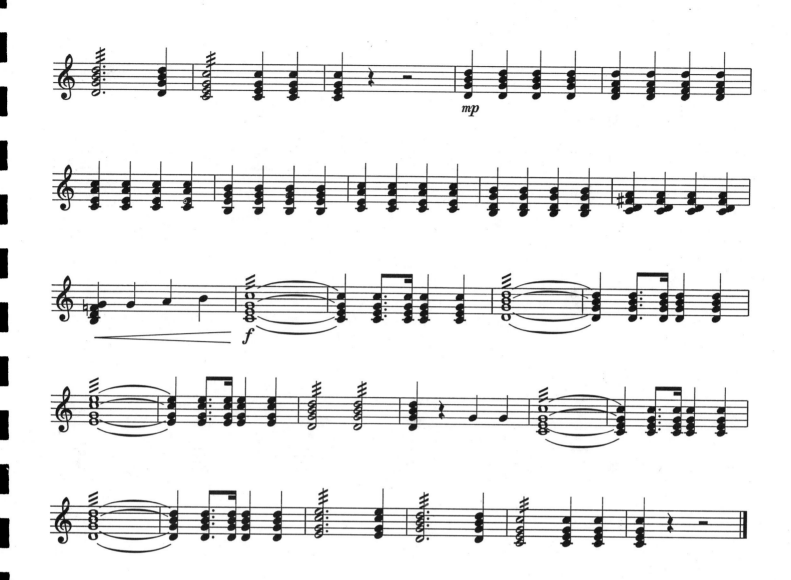

Study No. 3

Study No. 4

Study No. 5

Study No. 6

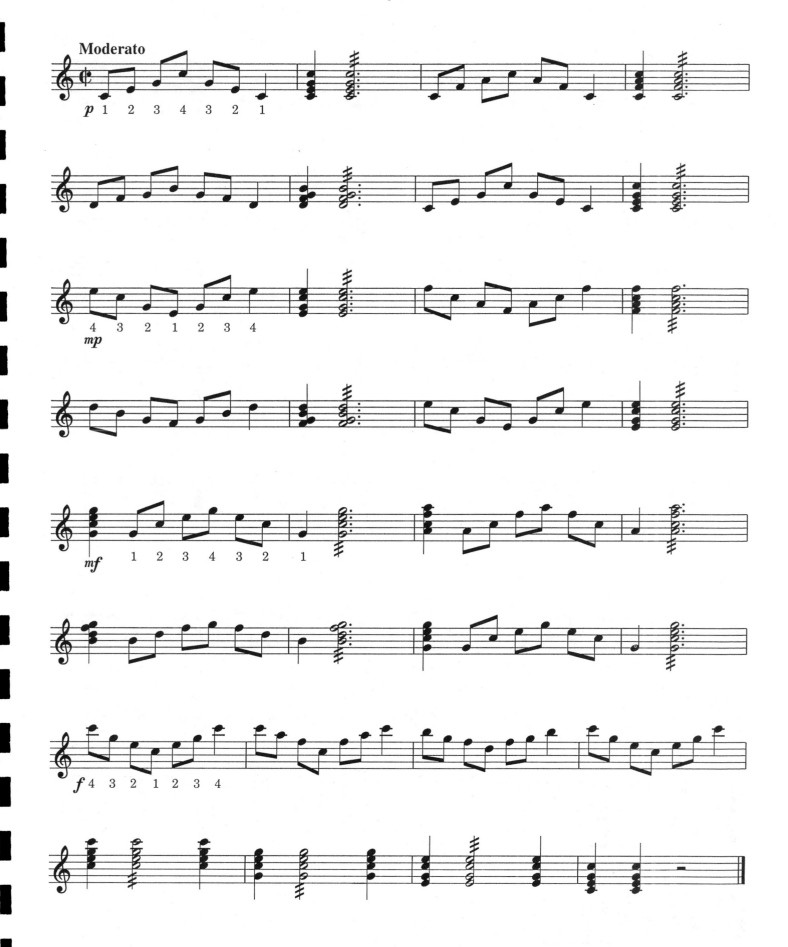

Study No. 7

Study No. 8

Study No. 9

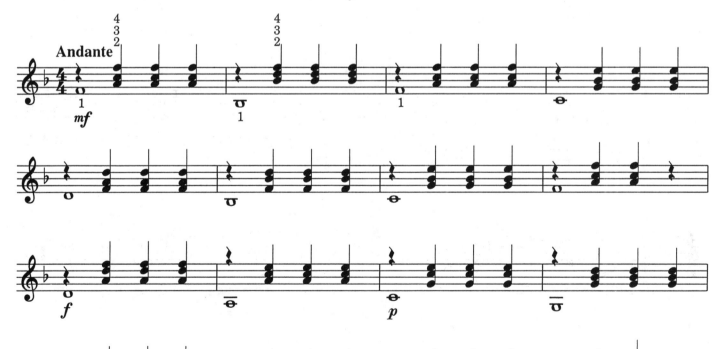

Study No. 10

Study No. 11

Study No. 12

Study No. 13

Study No. 14

Study No. 15

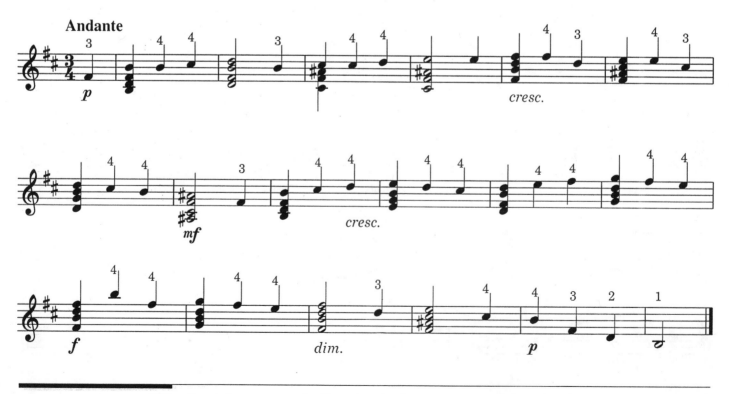

Study No. 16

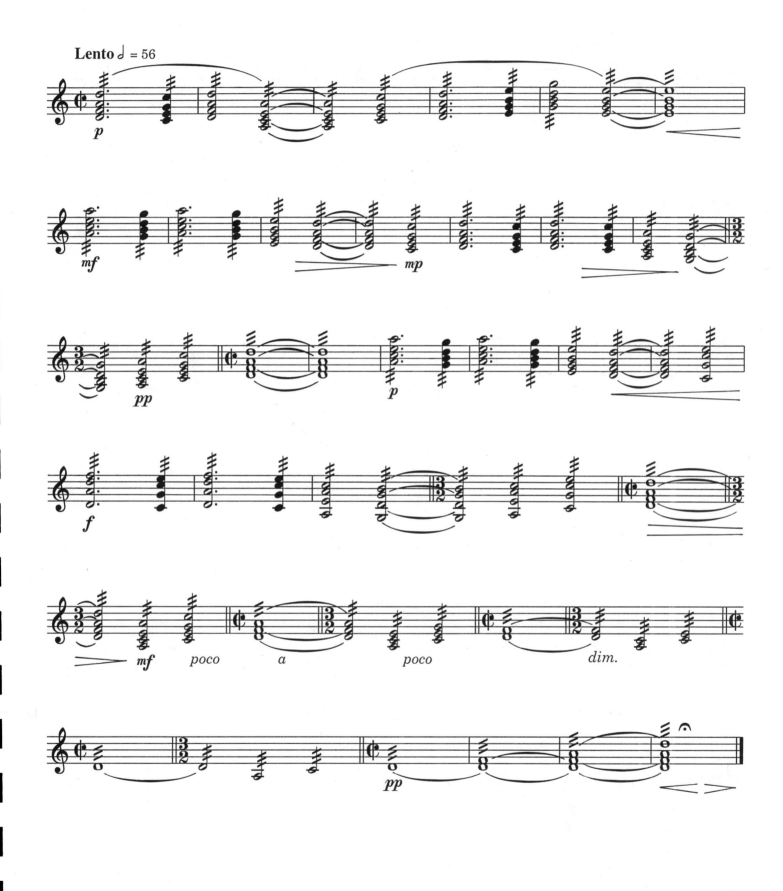

Study No. 17

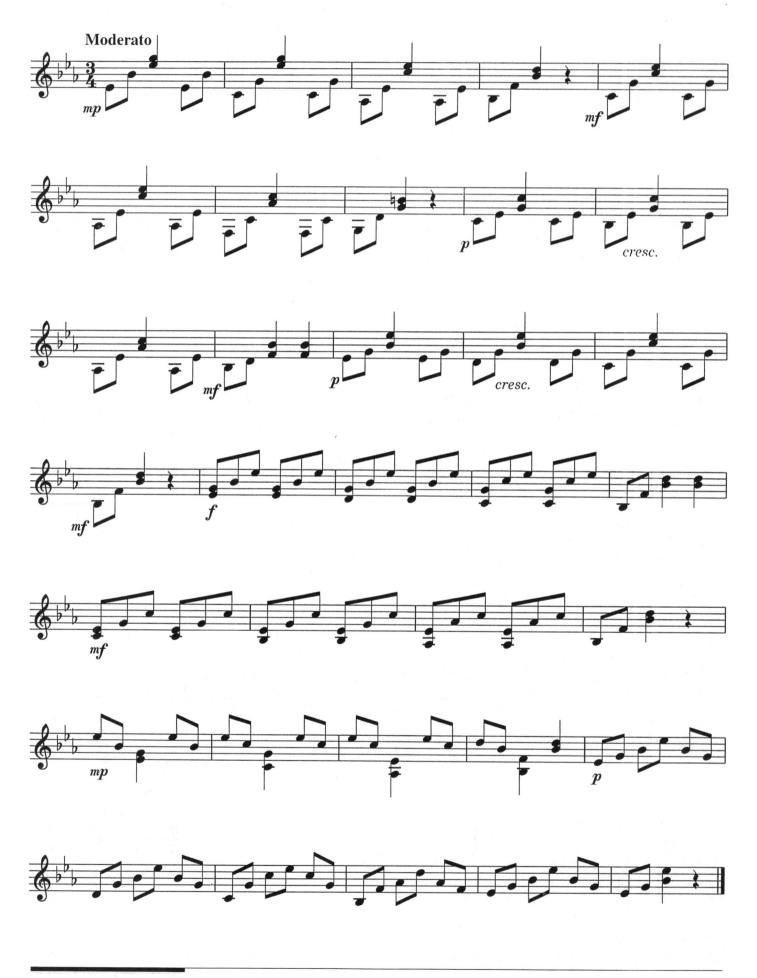

Study No. 18

Study No. 19

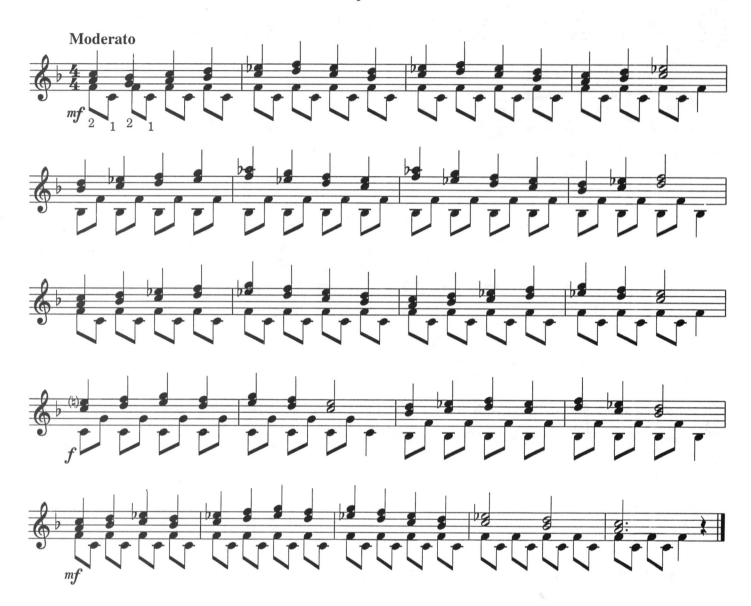

Study No. 20

Study No. 21

Study No. 22

Study No. 23

Study No. 24

Allegro

Stems Up = R.H.
Stems Down = L.H.

Study No. 25

Moderato